THE CONTEMPORARY JAPANESE ECONOMY

THE CONTEMPORARY JAPANESE ECONOMY

Yutaka Kosai

and

Yoshitaro Ogino

Translated by Ralph Thompson

Routledge
Taylor & Francis Group

LONDON AND NEW YORK

First published 1984 by M.E. Sharpe

Reissued 2018 by Routledge
2 Park Square, Milton Park, Abingdon, Oxon OX14 4RN
711 Third Avenue, New York, NY 10017, USA

Routledge is an imprint of the Taylor & Francis Group, an informa business

A Library of Congress record exists under LC control number: 84001241

ISBN 13: 978-1-138-04515-6 (hbk)
ISBN 13: 978-1-138-04512-5 (pbk)
ISBN 13: 978-1-315-1-77940 (ebk)

To Hisako, Fusae and Kinuko

Contents

Preface

This book is adapted from *Nihon Keizai Tembo*, published in Japanese in 1980 by Nihon Hyoronsha. The original Japanese version consisted of eighteen chapters, while the present book contains only eight. We have tried to summarize the main discussions of the original version. In some places data have been updated, and in others material has been added. Some institutional and other explanations have also been inserted in order to help foreign readers, often upon suggestions from the translator.

The first three chapters discuss macroeconomic trends in the Japanese economy since the end of the Second World War, features of the High Economic Growth Period of 1955–70, and how it changed to more moderate growth in the 1970s. The high rate of savings, the changing pattern in business cycles and capital accumulation are among the main topics.

The succeeding three chapters deal with the 'microeconomic foundation' of the economy – the working of industrial and financial organizations. Confronted with a considerable decline in economic growth, and significant changes in the role of the Japanese economy in the world market, industrial and financial organizations had to adjust and adapt. Our task is to ascertain what changed and what remain unchanged. Our interpretation is that, contrary to the widely held notion of the directed economy, 'Japan, Inc.', the Japanese economy is a competitive, market-oriented economy, and is becoming increasingly more so. The market concentration ratio reveals no definite rising trend; small industries survive and a liberalization of financial regulations is taking place.

The final two chapters cover socio-political aspects of the contemporary Japanese economy. Economic policy is formed, under pressure from competing domestic groups, with the government having limited freedom of action due to the international situation and Japan's position in it. The view of complete domination by big business and bureaucrats seems to be inaccurate.

In short, this book is an exercise in applied economics; it looks at the interplay of market forces in the Japanese economy. The authors' intention is to provide a guidebook of the Japanese economy, to give a picture of the overall trends. Statistical figures and tables and summaries of some of the main debates among Japanese economists are also included for the reader's information.

YUTAKA KOSAI
YOSHITARO OGINO

Translator's Note

I would like to acknowledge help from the following: Michael Roach for his help with the economics; Hideo Yamashita for his help with the Japanese; and co-author Yutaka Kosai for his wholehearted co-operation.

RALPH THOMPSON

1 High Economic Growth, 1955-70

1.1 INTRODUCTION

During the period 1955-70 the Japanese economy achieved an annual growth rate, in real terms, of about 10 per cent. In Japan we now refer to these years as the High Economic Growth Period (hereafter referred to as HEGP).

Our principal aims in this chapter are: first, to examine the distinctive characteristics of HEGP using macro economic theory, in an attempt to discover the facts behind them; and second, to discuss the interrelationship of those facts. By doing this we hope to throw light upon the 'mechanism' of high growth, and at the same time establish a starting point for a discussion of economic trends in Japan since HEGP. In this chapter we concentrate on the following four features of HEGP:

(a) the rate of growth accelerated as the period progressed;
(b) the capital coefficient remained low;
(c) investment rose sharply, to very high levels;
(d) the rate of personal savings also rose very sharply.

We may note also some other characteristics of HEGP:

(e) wholesale prices were almost constant, while consumer prices rose gradually (at about 5 per cent annually, after 1960);
(f) labour's share of the national income rose very slightly;
(g) the distribution of income became more equal (particularly between employees of small companies and those of large companies);
(h) until 1965 the government successfully balanced the budget;
(i) Japan's international balance of payments figures gradually changed from a deficit to a surplus.

Points (e)-(i) will be discussed in detail in later chapters, but we also refer to them wherever necessary in this chapter.

1

Finally, we should like to emphasize that in this chapter we are treating the Japanese economy as an isolated unit. We discuss only internal elements, leaving international considerations until later.

1.2 HOW HIGH WAS THE GROWTH RATE?

According to the Economic Planning Agency's National Income Statistics, Japan's annual growth rate, in real terms, for the period 1955–70 was 10.2 per cent. Broken down further, it was 8.5 per cent for 1955–60, 9.8 per cent for 1960–5, and 11.2 per cent for 1965–70 (see Table 1.1). In other words, it was gaining momentum as time went on.

That these growth rates were indeed extremely high can be seen from comparisons with Japan's growth rate before the Second World war, the ten years after the war, and with the growth rates of other advanced

TABLE 1.1 Japan's economic growth rate, capital coefficient, and investment ratio, 1951–80

Period (fiscal years)	1951–5	1955–60	1960–5	1965–70	1970–5	1975–80
Economic growth rate	7.6	8.5	9.8	11.2	4.7	4.9
[a] Capital coefficient A	2.2	2.5	2.9	2.9	7.3	6.6
Capital coefficient B	1.0	1.3	1.5	1.6	3.7	3.3
[b] Investment ratio A	16.7	21.2	28.2	32.6	34.4	32.3
Investment ratio B	8.0	11.2	14.9	17.8	17.5	16.0

Notes:
The Keizai Kikakuchō (Economic Planning Agency) *Kokumin Shotoku Tōkei* (National Income Statistics) are divided into two series, the *Kyūsuikei* (Old Estimates), covering 1946–76 (which conform to the 1953 UN System of National Accounts) and the *Shinsuikei* (New Estimates) for the years since 1965 (which conform to the 1968 UN System of National Accounts). There is of course some overlapping, and there are breaks and discontinuities. Unless otherwise specified, the figures in this chapter are taken from the Old Estimates.
[a] Capital coefficient = investment ratio ÷ economic growth rate.
[b] Investment ratio A = gross fixed capital formation ÷ GNE;
Investment ratio B = gross fixed private business capital formation ÷ GNE.
Sources:
Economic growth rate 1951–70 – Keizai Kikakuchō (Economic Planning Agency), *Kokumin Shotoku Tōkei Nenpō* (*Kyūsuikei* – Old Estimates), Ōkurashō Insatsukyoku (Government Printing Office), 1976, p. 7 (at 1970 prices); economic growth rate 1970–81 – Keizai Kikakuchō (Economic Planning Agency), *Kokumin Keizai Keisan Nenpō* (*Shinsuikei* – New Estimates), Ōkurashō Insatsukyoku (Government Printing Office), Dec. 1981 (at 1975 prices).

countries (see Table 1.2). There is some controversy over Japan's over-all growth rate since the Meiji Restoration in 1868,[1] but no one disputes the fact that the HEGP growth rate was significantly higher than that of the period before the Second World War. Statistics for the period following the Second World War tend to be unreliable, but Japan's growth rate for 1946–55 has been estimated at 8.9 per cent (Table 1.2). This is of course very high, but this period can be regarded as an exceptional case, because of the prevailing 'recovery conditions'. The chaos that came with defeat in the war caused a very sharp fall in production during the period immediately after the war, and it is not altogether surprising, therefore, that when the country settled down there was a sharp recovery period until previous economic levels were reached.

TABLE 1.2 Domestic and international comparison of economic growth rates

Country – period		Growth rate %	Source
Japan	1889–1938	3.2	Ohkawa estimates[a]
Japan	1946–55	8.9	Estimates of national income – Old Series[b]
Japan	1955–70	10.2	Table 1.1
Japan	1970–80	4.8	Table 1.1
USA	1960–70	3.9	OECD[c]
West Germany	1960–70	4.7	OECD
France	1960–70	5.6	OECD
UK	1960–70	2.8	OECD

Notes:
[a] Kazushi Ohkawa *et al.*, *Kokumin Shotoku*, Tōyō Keizai Shinpōsha, 1974.
[b] Keizai Kikakuchō (Economic Planning Agency), *Gendai Nihon Keizai no Tenkai*, 1976, p. 578.
[c] OECD's national accounts of OECD countries.

By 1955, however, these special conditions no longer prevailed, and a fall in the growth rate would have caused no surprise. In fact, growth continued at a similar level until 1970. Most advanced industrial nations achieved a higher growth rate after the war than before, but the statistics for 1950–70 show that Japan's was significantly higher than any of the others.

In the 1970s Japan's growth rate fell considerably. A recent estimate for 1970–80 is a mere 4.8 per cent, and we think we can safely say that high economic growth is over, at least for the present. The end of high growth has brought home to us forcibly how remarkable HEGP's actually was.

1.3 LOW CAPITAL COEFFICIENT

The capital coefficient can be defined as the extra amount of capital stock required to produce one unit of national income. In other words:

$$\text{Average capital coefficient} = \frac{\text{capital stock}}{\text{GNP}}$$

$$\text{Marginal capital coefficient} = \frac{\text{amount of increase in capital stock}}{\text{amount of increase in GNP}}$$

Compared with other countries, Japan's marginal capital coefficient was low during HEGP (Table 1.3). The figures for five-year periods (Table 1.1) show that it did rise, but only slightly. The average capital coefficient fell during 1955–60, and rose after that, but until 1970 the rise was very gradual (Table 1.4).

TABLE 1.3 International comparison of economic growth rates, capital coefficients and investment ratios, 1965–70

	Japan	USA	West Germany	France	UK
Economic growth rate G	11.2	3.2	4.7	5.6	2.2
Capital coefficient C	2.9	4.4	5.3	4.8	8.2
Investment ratio S	32.6	14.1[a]	25.0	27.2	18.0

Note:
[a] USA's investment ratio does not include government fixed investment.
Sources:
Figures for Japan are taken from Table 1.1; figures for other countries are from Bank of Japan's international comparative statistics.

From Harrod's growth model $GC = s$ (G = economic growth rate, C = capital coefficient, s = savings), it is clear that a low capital coefficient is advantageous for high growth. This relationship between capital coefficient and growth drew the attention of many Japanese economists in 1960, when it was one of the vital points in the discussions on Japan's growth potential, and on Prime Minister Ikeda's government's plan to double the national income.[2] Most economists believed that the capital coefficient would rise sharply, and that the growth rate would fall correspondingly. One exception was Osamu Shimomura, who forecast that the capital coefficient would remain fairly constant. His views were sharply criticized by such economists as Shigeto Tsuru and Saburo Okita, and a heated debate ensued. But the historical

TABLE 1.4 Average capital coefficient and related statistics (at 1970 prices)

	1955	1960	1965	1970	1975
Average capital coefficient $\dfrac{K}{Y}$	1.11	1.07	1.12	1.17	1.45
Capital equipment per person employed (Unit – ¥ 1000) $\dfrac{K}{L}$	492	638	989	1643	2714
Average productivity (Unit – ¥ 1000) $\dfrac{Y}{L}$	443	596	883	1404	1867

Sources:
Private business gross fixed capital stock (*K*) – Keizai Kikakuchō Kokumin Shotokubu (Economic Planning Agency, National Income Dept), *Kokumin Keizai Keisan*, no. 31. Labour force (*L*) – from national censuses.
Y and *K* for 1975 computed from Keizai Kikakuchō (Economic Planning Agency), *Kokumin Keizai Keisan Nenpō, Shinsuikei*, Ōkurashō Insatsukyoku (Government Printing Office).

record shows that Shimomura's view was closer to the actual course of events (Tables 1.3 and 1.4).

The economists who thought that the capital coefficient would rise gave three reasons:

1. In Japan, immediately before and during the war, the stock of capital equipment had been built up very considerably. In the ten years after the war, production could be expanded simply by taking advantage of this, and new large-scale investment was unnecessary. It was this, they said, that had kept the marginal capital coefficient low. By 1960, however, these reserves of capital were virtually exhausted, and any increase in production would require a massive new wave of investment. Therefore, they said, a rise in the capital coefficient was inevitable.

2. In Japan's industrial structure of the future, they said, capital-intensive heavy industries would be increasingly important. This would bring about an increase in the scale of investment, and consequently in 'company investment not directly concerned with production' ('Kansetsu Bumon Tōshi' – a major item in Japan,

because as well as office buildings, etc., companies often provide housing, and a variety of social and sporting facilities for their employees).
3. They believed that Japan's capital coefficient would rise to international levels, simply because it was much lower than the international average.

Of these three, we think that there was a certain amount of truth in (1). In the case of (2), however, what actually happened – the scale of investment and the degree of capital intensity did rise, but without a corresponding increase in the capital coefficient – indicates that their conclusions were mistaken. As for (3), we think that they overlooked the fact that there are inherent differences in the economies of different countries, which would be reflected in the capital coefficient.

In summary we would say that the majority group of economists were correct in forecasting that the capital coefficient would rise, but they greatly overestimated the size and speed of the rise, with the result that their calculations on how long high growth could continue were mistaken.

We must ask ourselves, then, why did the capital coefficient remain comparatively low for such a long period? One obvious answer is that the working ratio of capital equipment was high, but clearly we must delve a bit deeper than this. Let us examine three theories that have been put forward:

1. The first one stresses Japan's overpopulation and shortage of capital. It explains that the average capital coefficient (K/Y) is low when capital equipment per person employed (K/L) is low, in other words when the amount of capital in relation to the population is low.[3] This might be a persuasive hypothesis to explain the early years of HEGP, but as the period progressed capital intensity rose sharply, particularly after 1960 when a shortage of labour actually became one of the features of the economy.

2. A second theory is that the capital coefficient remained low because of an increase in productivity.

Average capital coefficiency $\dfrac{K}{Y}$

$= $ Capital Intensity $\dfrac{K}{L} \div$ Labour productivity $\dfrac{Y}{L}$

Thus, even if capital intensity increases, provided that productivity also increases the capital coefficient will remain low. Labour productivity did in fact increase significantly during HEGP, so it is quite conceivable that this prevented a sharp rise in the capital coefficient.

Let us express this another way, introducing a new element μ – the rate of technical progress. Thus $g = \mu + \alpha \times k + \beta \times l$ (g = growth rate, α = capital's share of national income, k = increase in capital stock, β = labour's share of national income, l = increase in labour supply).

Let us imagine an economy where $k = 12$ per cent, $l = 2$ per cent, $\mu = 5$ per cent, $\alpha = 0.3$ and $\beta = 0.7$. In such an economy the annual growth rate would be 10 per cent. The capital coefficient (k minus g) would increase by 1 per cent annually. In other words, if the average capital coefficient was 1.5, it would rise by only 0.01 or 0.02 annually. This is of course only a hypothetical example, but it is in fact similar to the actual state of the Japanese economy in the 1960s. (The actual figures, of course, go to several decimal places. In reality the figure of 5 per cent for μ would in fact have been nearer 4 per cent, but I use 5 for simplicity.)

3. The third theory concentrates on the composition of capital formation.[4] It states that in Japan the proportion of investment directly connected with production was high, while investment in areas such as pollution control and private housing, and social overhead capital, were comparatively low. This view has been rather influential in Japan. One problem is, however, that while we know that social overhead capital contributes indirectly to production, it is very difficult to measure that contribution. Also, it is not easy to compare the composition of capital formation in different countries, because industries that are private in some countries are government-run, or partly government-run in others, and also because, despite UN standards, statistical methods inevitably vary slightly. From that we do know, however, the proportion of investment directly connected with production in Japan does not seem to have been particularly high when compared with countries such as West Germany or France.

In fact, if anything, social overhead capital and investment in private housing in Japan appear to have been rather high compared with other countries. In any case, there does not seem to be sufficient evidence for theory (3). Theory (2) seems to be the most convincing, that is, that the main reason for the capital coefficient remaining low during HEGP was the increase in productivity.

1.4 THE INCREASE IN THE INVESTMENT RATIO

As can be seen from Table 1.1, gross fixed capital formation increased from 16.7 per cent of gross national expenditure for the period 1951–5 to 28.2 per cent for 1960–5, and 32.6 per cent for 1965–70. Table 1.5 further shows that by 1970 the proportion of National Income devoted to capital formation by both private and public sectors was greater than in other leading industrial countries.

TABLE 1.5 An international comparison of the composition of capital formation

| | *Japan* | | | | | *(All 1970)* | | | |
	1955	*1960*	*1965*	*1970*	*1975*	*USA*	*UK*	*West Germany*	*France*
Business fixed capital formation	7.7	14.0	13.3	20.0	17.1	10.3	14.6	17.1	15.4
Pollution control	0.1	0.2	0.2	0.5	1.7				
Private housing	3.4	4.4	6.1	6.6	6.8	3.2	1.6	5.4	6.6
Government fixed capital formation	5.3	6.6	8.8	8.6	8.8	—	2.1	3.9	3.5
Gross fixed capital formation	16.4	27.8	30.3	39.4	32.7	—	18.3	26.4	25.5

Sources:
For Japan, see Table 1.1
For other countries, see Bank of Japan's international comparative statistics. (Investment by government enterprises is included in business fixed capital formation.)

The core of this rise was a sharp increase in private investment in equipment. It rose from 8 per cent of GNP for 1951–5, to 14.9 per cent for 1960–5, and 17.8 per cent for 1965–70. This increase has been seen as one of the decisive influences on the growth rate during HEGP. It contributed in many ways:

1. It brought about a considerable increase in capacity.
2. It prevented a slackening of the growth rate due to labour shortage, particularly after 1960, by the substitution of capital for labour.
3. It enabled the introduction of modern equipment into industry, strengthening Japan's ability to compete internationally. This, in turn,

reduced the extent to which balance of payments problems acted as a ceiling on the expansion of the economy.
4. Expenditure on investment stimulated over-all demand directly and indirectly through the multiplier effect. The average annual increase of private investment in equipment, 17.2 per cent, was well above the increase in over-all demand during HEGP, particularly during the periods 1955–60 and 1965–70 (Table 1.6).

TABLE 1.6 Growth rates by demand category

Fiscal years	1951–5	1955–60	1960–5	1965–70	1970–5	1975–80
Real gross national expenditure	7.8	8.5	9.8	11.2	4.7	4.9
Private consumption expenditure	9.5	7.7	9.2	9.3	5.4	3.6
Private housing construction	14.6	14.0	18.4	15.5	6.1	−0.2
Business fixed capital formation	8.2	19.1	8.8	19.3	0.7	5.8
Government expenditure	4.2	5.7	10.6	7.4	6.0	4.3
Exports of goods and services	8.5	11.6	15.1	16.3	11.1	10.6
Imports of goods and services	13.7	14.0	12.2	16.5	5.9	5.2

Sources:
For 1951–70 – Keizai Kikakuchō (Economic Planning Agency), *Kokumin Shotoku Tōkei Nenpō 1951–70*, Ōkurashō Insatsukyoku (Government Printing Office), Dec 1972.
For 1970–80 – Keizai Kikakuchō (Economic Planning Agency), *Kokumin Keizai Keisan Nenpo, Shinsuikei 1980*, Okurashō Insatsukyoku (Government Printing Office), Dec 1981.

These four points suggest that the role played by private investment was extremely important. Growth accounting, however, suggests that its contribution to growth was not necessarily so great. Let us take an example where the growth rate = 10 per cent, the increase in capital stock = 10 per cent, the increase in the labour force = 2 per cent, capital's share of national income = 0.3, and of labour's share 0.7. In this case the contribution of capital savings would be 3 per cent (10 × 0.3) and of labour 1.4 per cent (2 × 0.7). (The figures for the growth rate, capital share, and labour share are approximations of those for HEGP.)

The remaining 5.6 per cent (10–3–1.4) is assumed to be the contribution of technical progress. In reality, however, this is an area that economists really know little about, and it might better be called the residual factor.

Hisao Kanamori's[5] and Denison and Chung's[6] work on labour input produced rather similar results. Their calculations (on the effects of changes in working hours, sex, age, and quality of labour, education, and investment patterns) also suggested that the 'residual factor' contributed the most to growth. Kanamori emphasizes that while the contribution of capital accumulation in Japan was large compared with other countries, it was belittled by the technical progress factor.

Was investment's contribution extremely important then, or was it less important, as growth accounting suggests? Rather than supporting one view or the other, let us try to reconcile them somewhat, by taking a look at the quality of capital input. For this purpose we will take a look at the so-called 'embodiment hypothesis'.[7] This states that the fact that new capital equipment embodies technical innovation was of the utmost importance. Thus an increase in investment not only increases the amount of capital stock, it also rejuvenates it and improves its quality, enabling significant technical improvement. The statistics provided by the Economic Planning Committee ('Keizai Shingikai Kikaku Iinkai', an advisory organ to the Prime Minister) give an idea of the extent of rejuvenation. According to them, the average age of capital stock in 1955 was 16.5 years. By 1960 this had been reduced to 9.4 years and by 1970, 7.2 years.[8]

In Table 1.7 this factor and the calculations of growth accounting have

TABLE 1.7 A breakdown of the main elements of growth, 1955—70

	%
Growth rate	10.2
Labour force	1.5
Employees	1.9
Working hours	Δ 0.3
Quality of labour	0.5
Capital	4.8
Capital stock	10.4
Quality of capital	5.7
Basic technical progress	3.9

Sources:
Keizai Seichō by Yutaka Kōsai and Seiichi Toshida (based on Toshida's research), Nihon Keizai Shinbunsha, 1981, pp. 168–72.
Quality of labour – Rōdōshō (Ministry of Labour), *Chingin Kōzō Kihon Chōsa.*
Quality of capital – Keizai Shingikai Kikaku Iinkai, 'Shōwa 50 Nendai no Senzai Seichōryoku to sono Mondaiten, in Keizai Kikakuchō (Economic Planning Agency), *Atarashii Keizai Keikaku,* 1976.

been incorporated and an attempt made to measure the various contributions to growth. This table suggests that the effective increase in capital was more than 50 per cent greater than the simple increase in capital stock, and the rejuvenation of capital contributed more to growth even than basic technical progress.

1.5 PERSONAL SAVINGS

As can be seen from Figure 1.1, personal saving increased at almost the same rate as private investment in equipment. Here we will not take up the question of why personal saving was high in Japan, but rather look at the speed of the rise, the level it rose to, and its contribution to high growth.

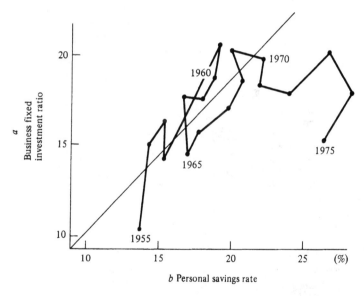

FIGURE 1.1 Equipment investment and the personal savings rate

Notes:
a Business fixed investment ratio = business fixed investment ÷ GNP;
b Personal savings rate = personal savings ÷ personal disposable income.

Source:
Keizai Kikakuchō (Economic Planning Agency) , *Kokumin Shoboku Tōkei*, Ōkurashō Insatsukyoku (Government Printing Office), 1977.

Personal savings increased from 13.4 per cent in 1955 to 20.4 per cent in 1970, a much higher rate of increase than in other advanced industrial countries (see Table 1.8). According to the survey of households by the Prime Minister's Office, Statistics Bureau (Sōrifu Tōkeikyoku) the rate of saving by households of persons employed was almost the same whether examined in time series, or by a cross-section of income levels. This is an indication of just how fast personal savings did in fact rise during HEGP, because usually a rise appears to be greater when examined by the latter method than the former (see Figure 1.2). During HEGP the propensity to invest was very high, so that if savings had not been correspondingly high, inflation and international balance of payments difficulties would have ensued. In an economy where measures have to be taken constantly to curb inflation or rectify a balance of payments deficit, the desired rate of investment is seldom achieved, and growth is retarded.

TABLE 1.8 An international comparison of personal savings levels

	1960	*1970*	*1975*
Japan	17.3	20.0	24.9
USA	4.9	8.2	8.5
UK	4.7	5.6	10.0
West Germany	14.9	16.6	14.5
France	9.7	16.9	17.7
South Korea	Δ 1.3	4.5	5.0

Source:
Keizai Kikakuchō Khosakyoku (Economic Planning Agency's Research Bureau), *Kokusai Keizai Yōran*, 1978.

Personal savings is, however, only one branch of savings. An increase in government and company savings would also serve to maintain the balance between savings and investment, and during HEGP they both increased significantly (see Table 1.9). Nevertheless we feel that the role of personal savings was very important, because without it a much bigger change in the relative shares of profits and wages would have been necessary to bring about the same level of investment, and such changes are not easy to make. We will illustrate this with our own application of a model introduced by Kaldor.[9] First let us divide GNP, or Y, into Y^D (personal disposable income) and Y^R (retained income, i.e. GNP minus personal disposable income) and call savings from Y^D and Y^R, S_D and S_R

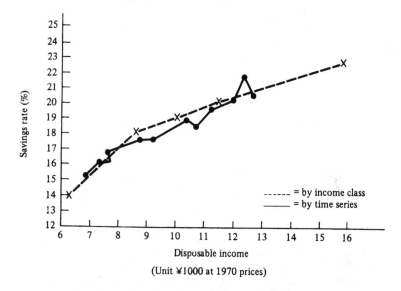

FIGURE 1.2 The savings rate for households of persons employed

Source:
Sōrifu Tōkeikyoku (Prime Minister's Office, Statistics Bureau), *Kakei Chōsa Nenpō*, Nihon Tōkei Kyōkai, 1965–75.

TABLE 1.9 Sources of savings

(Unit – thousand billion yen)	1955	1960	1965	1970	1975
Personal savings	0.9	1.9	3.8	9.6	27.4
Corporate retained earnings	0.2	1.0	1.0	4.8	3.0
Government savings	0.4	1.2	2.0	5.6	2.8
Depreciation provisions	0.8	1.7	4.2	9.9	18.5
External surplus (−)	Δ0.1	0.0	Δ 0.4	Δ 0.8	Δ 0.0

Source:
Keizai Kikakuchō (Economic Planning Agency), *Kokumin Shotoku Tōkei Nenpō Kyūsuikei* and *Kokumin Keizai Keisan Nenpō, Shinsuikei*.

respectively. In order for savings to be equal to investment, therefore:

$$I = S_D Y^D + S_R Y^R$$

Hence, $\dfrac{Y^R}{Y} = \dfrac{1}{S_R - S_D}\left(\dfrac{I}{Y}\right) - \dfrac{S_D}{S_R - S_D}$

Usually it is safe to assume that $S_R > I/Y > S_D$. Assuming that this is in fact the case, in order to obtain a level of savings necessary to produce an increase in investment, the ratio of retained income to GNP must increase and that of personal disposable income decrease:

$$\frac{\partial\left(\dfrac{Y^R}{Y}\right)}{\partial\left(\dfrac{I}{Y}\right)} = \frac{1}{S_R - S_D} > 0$$

For a situation where an increase in personal savings is achieved without an increase in retained income, the equation would be:

$$\frac{\partial\left(\dfrac{Y^R}{Y}\right)}{\partial S_D} = \frac{1}{(S_R - S_D)^2}\left(\frac{I}{Y} - S_R\right) < 0$$

Let us illustrate these relationships using real statistics from Table 1.10. Between 1955 and 1970 the investment ratio rose from 25 per cent to 39 per cent.

If personal savings had remained at their 1955 level, retained income would have had to rise to 42 per cent. In fact, because the level of personal savings rose from 13 per cent in 1955 to 20 per cent in 1970, a retained

TABLE 1.10 The savings rate, investment, retained income and GNP

	Investment ratio $\dfrac{I}{Y}$	Personal savings rate S_D	Ratio of savings to retained income S_R	Ratio of retained income to GNP $\dfrac{YR}{Y}$
1955	0.25	0.13	0.57	0.26
1960	0.35	0.16	0.83	0.33
1965	0.33	0.17	0.66	0.32
1970	0.39	0.20	0.74	0.35
Hypothetical	(0.39)	(0.13)	(0.74)	(0.42)
1975	0.32	0.25	0.54	0.24

Note:
Retained income = GNP − personal disposable income.
Source:
Keizai Kikakuchō (Economic Planning Agency), *Kokumin Shotoku Tōkei Nenpō*, *Kyūsuikei* and *Kokumin Keizai Keisan Nenpō*, *Shinsuikei*.

income level of 35 per cent was sufficient to produce that level of investment.

If the relative shares of profits and wages could change freely, even if personal savings did not rise, the government and companies could create enough savings between them to meet investment needs, and personal savings would not be such an important factor in economic growth. In reality, however, it is no easy matter for the government, or for companies, to increase savings. To increase government savings requires a tax increase or cuts in government expenditure, and either of these measures would of course meet with political opposition. As for company savings, changes in the shares of profits and wages are limited by technical factors. To illustrate this let us introduce the elasticity of substitution between capital and labour, δ. If

$$\delta = \frac{d\left(\dfrac{K}{L}\right)}{\dfrac{K}{L}} \div \frac{d\left(\dfrac{W}{r}\right)}{\dfrac{W}{r}},$$

changes in capital's share of national income α, and changes in capital stock per capital $d(K/L)$, will be related in the following way:[10]

$$d\alpha = (1 - \alpha)\left(1 - \frac{1}{\delta}\right)d\left(\frac{K}{L}\right)$$

Therefore, unless the value of δ is near to zero, there will be no great change in the relative shares of capital and labour. When $\delta = 1$ (as in the Cobb–Douglas production function) even if there is an increase in capital accumulation (K/L) the shares will remain constant. For the capital share to be affected by such an increase, the value of δ must be less than 1.

According to Denison's estimates,[11] Japan's capital share rose from 22.4 per cent for the period 1952–9, to 27.1 per cent for 1960–71, an annual increase of 2 per cent. Assuming capital stock per capita (K/L) increased at about 8 per cent annually, according to the above model δ would be 1.4. Thus the capital share rose, but not to such a great extent, particularly when compared with the increase in capital stock. Without the increase in personal savings it would have been very difficult to maintain the balance between savings and investment.

1.6 THE RELATIVE PRICE OF INVESTMENT GOODS AND CONSUMPTION GOODS

One factor that caused savings and hence investment to rise, and thereby contributed to high growth, was the change in the relative price of investment goods and consumption goods, or to put it another way, the change in the 'terms of trade' between personal savings and company savings.

To illustrate this,[12] we will call Y (GNP) nominal national income, I (investment) nominal investment, and P_Y, P_I the deflators for national income and investment.

Thus real growth,

$$G = \frac{\Delta \frac{Y}{P_Y}}{\frac{Y}{P_Y}}$$

Capital coefficient,

$$C = \frac{\frac{I}{P_I}}{\Delta \frac{Y}{P_Y}}$$

If personal savings only took place, and the only concern of households was consumer prices P_C, the rate of savings s would become

$$\frac{\frac{S}{P_C}}{\frac{Y}{P_C}} = \frac{S}{Y}$$

(S/Y = nominal savings rate). Setting $P = P_I/P_Y$ we have $GC = P_S$. In this case P expresses the terms under which savings are transferred from households to companies.

What will happen, then, if investment goods become cheaper than consumption goods? Even if the nominal amount of savings is the same, the amount of investment goods purchased will increase. Therefore even if the investment ratio is the same as that of savings, it is possible for investment to increase. During HEGP the relative price of investment goods did in fact fall. The deflator for GNP during HEGP increased by

4.6 per cent annually, while the deflator for private investment in equipment rose by only 2.2 per cent annually.

A comparison of 1955–60 and 1965–70 (Table 1.11) reveals that the growth rate was 2.8 per cent higher annually, and the capital coefficient 1.5 per cent higher annually in the later period. Thus real investment was 4.3 per cent (2.8 + 1.5) greater, while nominal savings increased by only 1.8 per cent. The balance was made up by the 2.4 per cent change in the relative price of investment goods and consumption goods. Its contribution to growth was therefore very significant.

TABLE 1.11 The change in the relative price of investment goods and consumption goods, 1955–60 and 1965–70

	Growth rate (A)	Capital coefficient (B)	Relative price (C)	Nominal Savings rate (D)
1955–60	8.5	2.764	0.758	31.4
1965–70	11.2	3.187	0.965	37.5
Rate of change	2.8	1.5	2.4	1.8

Notes:
(A), (B) at 1970 prices, (D) at current prices.
(A) × (B) = (C) × (D).
Source:
Keizai Kikakuchō (Economic Planning Agency), *Kokumin Shotoku Tōkei Nenpō*, *Kyūsuikei*.

During HEGP wholesale prices remained almost constant, while consumer prices rose. This corresponded with the change in the relative price of investment and consumption goods. These price changes were the result of high economic growth, and at the same time the conditions which supported its continuance.

1.7 THE END OF HEGP

During HEGP the tendency was for the growth rate to gain momentum. By the late 1960s, however, it was approaching its limit. Gross capital formation had reached a remarkable 40 per cent of GNP, and private investment in equipment and personal savings had both reached 20 per cent. It would have been difficult to imagine them increasing much more.

During the 1970s the Japanese economy experienced not merely an end to the acceleration in growth, but in fact a considerable fall in its growth rate. To find the reasons for this we must look at some international factors that limited the expansion of the economy, and that we have not covered in this chapter.

NOTES

1. For details of this discussion, see Takafusa Nakamura, *Senzenki Nihon Keizai Seichō no Bunseki*, Iwanami Shoten, 1971, pp. 2–5; and Ryōshin Minami, *Nihon no Keizai Hatten*, Tōyō Keizai Shinpōsha, 1981, pp. 59–62.
2. Most of the arguments from this discussion can be found in *Nihon Keizai no Seichōryoku. Shimomura Riron to sono Handan*, ed. and pub. Kinyūzaisei Jijō Kenkyūjo (Economic Planning Agency's Research Institute), *Shihon Sutokku to Keizai Seichō*, 1962, pp. 26–35°, and Ryūtarō Komiya, *Gendai Nihon Keizai Kenkyū*, Tokyo University Press, 1975, p. 12, note 17.
3. Komiya, *Gendai Nihon Keizai Kenkyū*, p. 14 (iii).
4. Ibid., p. 14 (iv).
5. Hisao Kanamori, 'Nihon Keizai no Seichōritsu wa naze takai ka?' in Keizai Kikakuchō Keizai Kenkyūjo, (Economic Planning Agency Research Institute), *Keizai Bunseki*, no. 31.
6. E. Denison and W. Chung, 'Economic Growth and its Source', in *Asia's New Giant – How the Japanese Economy Works*, ed. H. Patrick and H. Rosovsky, The Brookings Institution, 1976, esp. p. 94, Table 2.11.
7. R. Solow, 'Technical progress, Capital Formation, and Economic Growth', *American Economic Review*, May 1962.
8. Keizai Shingikai's 'Shōwa 50 Nendai no Senzai Seichōryoku to sono Mondaiten', in Keizai Kikakuchō (Economic Planning Agency), *Atarashii Keizai Kikaku*, 1976.
9. N. Kaldor, *Essays on Value and Distribution*, Duckworth, 1960, pp. 227–36.
10. This model was introduced by M. Bronfenbrenner in, 'A Note on Relative Shares and Elasticities of Substitution', *Journal of Political Economy*, June 1961. J. Kendrick and R. Satō used this model with data on the US economy, and came up with a figure of $\delta = 0.58$. See Kendrick and Satō, 'Factor Prices, Productivity, and Economic Growth', *American Economic Review*, Sept 1963.
11. Denison and Chung, 'Economic Growth and its Source', p. 85.
12. This section is adapted from *Shihon Keisū, Chochikuritsu, Sōtaikakaku* Yutaka Kōsai, Chūō Keizai, Dec 1969.

2 Business Cycles, International Balance of Payments and Inflation

2.1 INTRODUCTION

HEGP was of course not a continuous process of smooth consistent economic expansion. It consisted rather of a series of booms and recessions. In this chapter we try to do three things:

1. We attempt to show that the business cycles of HEGP were a combination of cyclical changes in plant and equipment investment and inventory investment, regulated by the balance of payments situation.
2. We discuss how, towards 1970, world-wide inflation caused the international balance of payments ceiling to rise, so that eventually it no longer acted as a check on the expansion of the economy, and how this resulted in inflation and unemployment becoming the new ceiling and floor for the business cycle.
3. We explain how the inflation of the 1970s was of a completely different nature to that of the 1960s.

In the appendices at the end of the chapter are summaries of two major discussions that have taken place in Japan concerning these problems (the 'Tenkeiki' discussions, on the future of investment as foreseen in 1962, and the discussions on 'Seisansei Kakusa Infureishon' – productivity differential inflation) and our own interpretation of the second of them. The discussion in this chapter is also closely connected with that on the economic stabilization policy in Chapter 8.

2.2 THE BUSINESS-CYCLE PATTERN

Table 2.1 shows the Economic Planning Agency's reference dates for the peaks and troughs of Japan's business cycles since the Second World War. These dates coincide almost exactly with where the diffusion index crosses the 50 per cent line (see Figure 2.1). They show that while the pattern was the same, the lengths of the cycles varied. For this period the average length of the expansion phase (from the trough to the peak) was thirty-four months, and for the recession phase (from the peak to the trough) thirteen months – in other words, forty-seven months for a full cycle. While the expansion phase varied considerably, the recession phase was always about one year. The last three cycles were rather longer than the earlier ones.

Business cycles tend to be self regulating but they can be controlled to some extent. When we compare the dates of the cycles with those of the government's stabilization measures (Table 2.2) (here we are referring in particular to changes in the bank rate, by the Bank of Japan) their interaction can be seen clearly. However, there is usually a lag between the introduction of tight money measures and the beginning of the recession phase, and also between the relaxing of these measures and the beginning of recovery. The length of this lag has also varied, but it appears to have been longer in the last three cycles.

We should not think of the business cycle as a single simple process, but rather as the result of a combination of different cycles. During HEGP the variations of length were largely the result of the interaction of the inventory investment cycle and the plant and equipment investment cycle, and the effect of the international balance of payments situation. What is usually recognized as the business cycle is in fact largely the inventory investment cycle. This can be corroborated by two factors:

1. The reference dates for the business cycle and the inventory investment cycle are virtually the same (Figure 2.2).
2. In the periods immediately after the peaks and troughs, the changes in inventory investment were largely responsible for changes in gross national expenditure (Table 2.3). This was especially true of the second, third and fourth cycles, when it could be said that the reductions in GNE were caused almost completely by the reduction in inventory investment.

What, then, was the role of plant and equipment investment? The differences in the lengths of the expansion phases were caused by the

TABLE 2.1 Reference dates for business cycles, 1951–75

	Trough	Peak	Trough	Expansion period (months)	Recession period (months)	Full cycle (months)
1st cycle	—	June 1951	June 1951	—	4	—
2nd cycle	Oct 1951	Jan 1954	Nov 1954	27	10	37
3rd cycle	Nov 1954	June 1957	June 1958	31	12	43
4th cycle	June 1958	Dec 1961	Oct 1962	42	10	52
5th cycle	Oct 1962	Oct 1964	Oct 1965	24	12	36
6th cycle	Oct 1965	Jul 1970	Dec 1971	57	17	74
7th cycle	Dec 1971	Nov 1973	Mar 1975	23	16	39
Average				34	13	47
2nd–4th average				33	11	44
5th–7th average				35	15	50

Source:
Keizai Kikakuchō (Economic Planning Agency), *Nihon Keizai Shihyō*, Dec 1976.

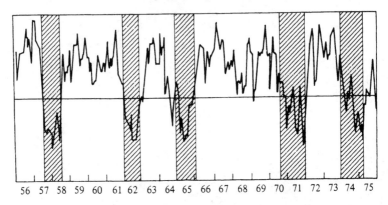

56 57 58 59 60 61 62 63 64 65 66 67 68 69 70 71 72 73 74 75

FIGURE 2.1 Diffusion index

Note:
The shaded section represents the recession period.
Source:
Keizai Kikakuchō (Economic Planning Agency) *Keizai Hendō Kansoku Shiryō Nenpō* (including an explanation of the methods involved in determining the diffusion index) and *Nihon Keizai Shihyō*, 1975.

TABLE 2.2 Reference dates for the government stabilization measures, 1957–75

	Adoption of tight money policy		Relaxation of tight money policy		Length of expansion period under tight money conditions (months)	Length of recession under relaxed money conditions (months)	Length of recession under tight money conditions (months)
3rd cycle	Mar	1957	June	1958	3	0	12
4th cycle	July	1961	Oct	1962	5	0	10
5th cycle	Mar	1964	Jan	1965	7	9	3
6th cycle	Sept	1969	Oct	1970	10	14	3
7th cycle	Apr	1973	Mar	1975	7	0	16

Note:
The discount rate was raised in 1959 and 1967, but it did not adversely affect business conditions.
Source:
The dates are based on changes in the Bank of Japan's official discount rate.

plant and equipment investment cycle. As can be seen from Table 2.4, the rate of plant and equipment investment was high for five years, and low for the next five years. When it was high, expansion continued even after inventory investment had tapered off, while when it was low expansion was very short-lived (e.g. the expansion phase of the 1962–5

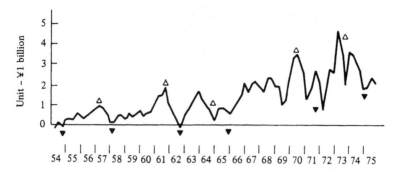

FIGURE 2.2 Changes in inventory investment, 1954–75

Note:
Δ = peak.
▼ = trough.
Source:
Keizai Kikakuchō, (Economic Planning Agency) *Kokumin Shotoku Tōkei Nenpō, Kyūsuikei* and *Kokumin Keizai Keisan Nanpō, Shinsuikei,* 1977.

TABLE 2.3 Changes in inventory investment compared with changes in total expenditure (at 1970 prices, unit ¥100 million)

	Early expansion period		Recession period	
	Total expenditure	Inventory investment	Total expenditure	Inventory investment
2nd cycle	24 489	8 324	Δ 4 380	Δ 5 937
3rd cycle	22 219	5 864	10 177	Δ 8 129
4th cycle	17 692	4 232	11 151	Δ 20 477
5th cycle	47 294	15 900	26 449	684
6th cycle	51 395	5 810	55 981	8 631
7th cycle	86 430	111	Δ 7 713	Δ 12 134

Note:
Early expansion period = first four quarters after the trough.
Source:
Keizai Kikakuchō (Economic Planning Agency), *Kokumin Shotoku Tōkei Nenpō, Kyūsuikei,* 1977.

business cycle). Although the level of plant and equipment investment varied during HEGP, the growth rate and the increase in the capital stock continued to rise steadily. In other words, to maintain approximately the same growth rate and increase in capital stock, a rate of

TABLE 2.4 Changes in the rate of increase in plant and equipment investment, 1955–75

	1955–60 %	1960–5 %	1965–70 %	1970–5 %
Rate of increase in plant and equipment investment	19.1	8.8	19.3	0.7
Economic growth rate	8.5	9.8	11.2	4.7
Rate of increase in capital stock	7.5	11.3	12.8	11.3
Investment ratio for first year of five-year period	7.7	14.0	13.3	20.9

Source:
Tables 1.4 and 1.6.

plant and equipment investment of almost 20 per cent greater than these two rates was necessary at certain times, while at other times considerably less than the other two was sufficient. This is of course the operation of the acceleration principle.

If the equipment investment ratio is low at the beginning of a particular period, a very sharp rise in equipment investment will be required to achieve a significant increase in the growth rate and the capital stock. This was certainly true of Japan's economy at the beginning of HEGP, as can be seen clearly from Table 2.4. Let us suppose that the plant and equipment investment ratio at the start of a particular period is less than the ideal, as calculated by:

Desired growth rate × Required capital coefficient

To achieve the desired growth rate, plant and equipment investment must rise sharply, to a rate of increase above the growth rate. In the opposite case, a fall in plant and equipment investment would be necessary. This relationship was particularly important during HEGP because (as was said in the discussion of the capital coefficient in Chapter 1) the growth rate of 1946–55 had been high because of two factors:

1. It was a period of recovery from the very sharp drop in production during the chaos immediately after the war.
2. It was possible to achieve a great deal simply by increasing the working ratio of the capital stock built up before and during the war. No new wave of investment had been necessary.

In contrast, the post-1955 period saw a massive increase in investment, more than was necessary in fact, so that it served to exaggerate the fluctuations of the business cycle.

2.3 THE CHANGE IN THE INTERNATIONAL BALANCE OF PAYMENTS SITUATION

During HEGP the balance of payments was the biggest single factor influencing economic growth and the business cycle. When the deficit grew, a tight money policy had to be adopted to correct it, and further economic expansion was temporarily sacrificed. During HEGP tight money measures were taken six times, three of which were caused by balance of payments deficits (1957, 1961 and 1964). Of the other three, two were relatively light preventive measures (1959 and 1967) which did not adversely affect business conditions. The general pattern – balance of payments deficit → tight money measures → recession – continued throughout most of HEGP. The last tight money measures (1969), however, were rather different, in that they were the first measures taken when there was a healthy balance of payments surplus. Their object was to curb inflation. There were two major reasons for the above pattern.

1. From 1949–71 the Japanese yen was fixed at ¥360 to the dollar.
2. Throughout most of this period Japan's foreign reserves were maintained at the minimum necessary level. In late 1955 Japan's foreign reserves were worth $700 million (equal to 3.6 months' imports). In late 1960 they had risen to $1800 million (= 4.9 months' imports) but in late 1965 they were only $2100 million (= 3.1 months' imports). It was not until after 1968 that they began to rise sharply.

In other words, Japan was putting all her efforts into increasing economic growth, and was not concerned about building up foreign reserves. As can be seen from Figure 2.3, while throughout most of the 1960s foreign reserves remained at around $2000 million, the supply of money was increasing steadily. Thus, when the balance of payments went into the red, and foreign reserves began to fall, there was no alternative but to tighten credit in order to curb domestic demand and maintain the fixed exchange rate. Furthermore, these measures were very effective in correcting the balance of payments situation. Part of the reason for this was that changes in the balance of payments were caused mainly by fluctuations in inventory investment, because it included a large amount of imports of raw materials. The rate of inventory investment reacted very quickly to stabilization measures. Expansion led to speculative accumulation of imported raw materials, which in turn led to a worsening of the balance of payments situation. When a tight money policy was adopted, production fell, accumulation of

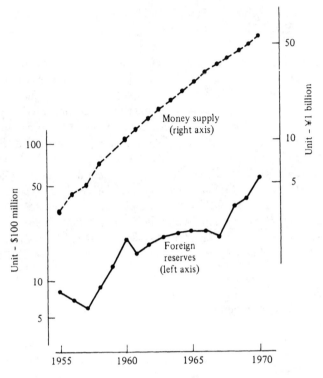

FIGURE 2.3 A comparison of foreign reserves and the supply of money, 1955–70

Note:
Money supply $= M_2$ (currency + demand deposits + time and savings deposits at commercial banks other than large certificates of deposits, i.e. USA definition).
Source:
Keizai Kikakuchō (Economic Planning Agency), *Keizai Yōran*, 1981.

imported raw materials stopped, and the balance of payments began to improve.

This situation, however, was gradually changing in the latter part of HEGP, and sharply towards the very end, in 1970. The reason for this was a fundamental change in the international balance of payments situation, so that it no longer acted as a ceiling on expansion. A look at Japan's balance of payments over the years since the war (Table 2.5) reveals that until the middle of the 1950s, a deficit on visible foreign trade

TABLE 2.5 Japan's international balance of payments figures, 1946-79

	1946–52	1953–7	1958–64	1965–70	1971–2	1973–5	1976–9
	(values – annual average, unit – $1 million)						
Visible trade balance	Δ 233	Δ 360	151	2 588	8 379	3 410	13 455
Exports	(661)	(2 041)	(4 480)	(12 601)	(25 799)	(48 522)	(85 547)
Imports	(894)	(2 401)	(4 329)	(10 013)	(17 740)	(45 111)	(72 091)
Invisible trade balance	100	211	Δ 304	Δ1 239	Δ1 810	Δ4 927	Δ7 202
Current balance	Δ133	Δ137	Δ 217	1 189	6 210	Δ1 830	5 622
Long-term balance of capital account	Δ 8	23	116	Δ 670	Δ2 784	Δ4 639	Δ7 384
Basic balance of payments	175	Δ114	Δ101	519	3 426	Δ6 476	Δ1 762
Short-term balance of capital account	17	33	85	303	2 783	Δ 54	1 750
Over-all balance	192	Δ 81	Δ 16	822	6 209	Δ6 530	Δ 11
Increase or decrease in foreign reserves	143	Δ 58	Δ211	400	6 983	Δ1 850	1 878
Financial account	49	Δ 23	Δ227	443	774	Δ4 680	Δ1 889

Sources:
For up to 1970– Keizai Kikakuchō, Chōsakyoku (Economic Planning Agency, Research Bureau), *Shiryō Keizai Hakusho 25 Nen*, Nihon Keizai Shinbunsha, 1972, p. 446.
For 1971 onwards–compiled from Ministry of Finance, Bank of Japan's balance of international payments figures.

was made up for by the surplus on invisible items such as services and transfer payments. From the second half of the 1950s invisible items began to show a deficit, but visible trade now showed an increasing surplus. In the late 1960s the visible trade surplus rose sharply, creating a considerable over-all surplus. Ironically, too great a surplus was beginning to be a problem. Then in 1973 the yen was put on a floating-exchange basis. That was the end of the balance of payments' role as a check on expansion.

Why was it that Japan's trade figures were able to climb out of the red, and eventually achieve a considerable surplus? There are of course several factors, but two are generally accepted as being the most important:

1. The increase in the ability of Japan's industries to compete internationally.
2. In a period of soaring world-wide inflation, Japan's prices remained relatively stable.

2.4 INFLATION – THE NEW CEILING FOR THE BUSINESS CYCLE

Between 1955 and 1960 both wholesale and consumer prices had been stable. After 1960 wholesale price remained almost the same, but consumer prices rose by about 5 per cent annually. In other words, during HEGP the Japanese economy was already experiencing sustained inflation (see Table 2.6). Various measures were taken to control consumer price inflation, but not a tightening of the money supply to reduce demand. This was because during HEGP inflation was not thought of as a ceiling for the business cycle, nor indeed did it act as one. Why was this?

First we must bear in mind that the inflation was of a very limited nature. It could not be described as 'total' inflation, because wholesale prices remained stable. While there was a change in absolute prices, the main change was in relative prices. Second, the rate of inflation was relatively low, low enough to allow a sharp rise in real incomes.

Let us assume, as we believe, that during HEGP the aim of government economic policies was, provided the fixed exchange rate could be maintained and international trade balanced, to increase the growth rate as much as possible. It is quite understandable, therefore, that they did not take measures to control the money supply. Stable

TABLE 2.6 Indicators of 'productivity differential inflation'

	(1) Wholesale price index (1970 = 100)	(2) Consumer price index (1970 = 100)	(3) Ratio of job offers to job seekers	(4) Wage differential %	(5) Productivity of national economy	(6) Productivity of manufacturing industries
1955	85.7	53.0	0.28	58.8	42.2	23.8
1960	88.0	57.1	0.62	58.9	59.0	36.9
1965	89.8	76.7	0.61	71.0	87.9	53.3
1970	100.0	100.0	1.35	69.6	141.6	100.0
Rate of change						
$\frac{1960}{1955}$	0.5	1.5	—	0.0	6.9	9.2
$\frac{1965}{1960}$	0.4	6.1	—	3.8	8.3	7.6
$\frac{1970}{1965}$	2.2	5.4	—	Δ 0.4	10.0	13.4

Sources:

(1)–(5)– Keizai Kikakuchō (Economic Planning Agency), *Gendai Nihon Keizai no Tenkai*, 1976.

Wage differential = $\dfrac{\text{average wage of companies with 30–99 employees}}{\text{average wage of companies with more than 500 employees}}$

(6)– Nihon Seisansei Honbu (Japan Productivity Centre), *Katsuyō Rōdō Tōkei*, 1976.

wholesale prices meant stable prices for exported industrial goods. Thus Japanese manufacturers' international competitiveness was maintained, and there was therefore no reason to take such measures. Great care was taken to prevent any further increase in consumer price inflation, which it was feared would raise wages to the extent that inflation would spread to the wholesale sector.

One might justifiably ask at this stage, did not consumer-price inflation cause social discontent and political protest? The answer is of course that it did, but not to the extent of the government being forced to take money supply control measures. There were three reasons for this:

1. The limited nature of inflation.
2. Fears about the effect such measures would have on growth, (and hence real incomes) and employment.
3. There was at this time great progress being made towards a fairer distribution of income. (This was of course closely linked with consumer-price inflation.)

During the 1950s there had been very large differences in wages in different industries, and between the wages paid by large and small companies. As Japan approached full employment in the 1960s, these differences were rapidly decreasing.

Wage rises in the old low-wage sectors – mostly small companies in labour-intensive industries – were pushing up their costs. Consumer prices rose because they included a high proportion of services, and the products of these small companies. On the other hand, wholesale prices, because they included a high proportion of industries with rapidly improving productivity, remained low (Table 2.7). This is what we call productivity differential inflation.

Of course the relative price change could have been achieved by keeping consumer prices stable and reducing wholesale prices or, to put it another way, by stable nominal wage levels and a rise in real wages. However, as we said above, government policy was to increase growth as much as possible, so that a tight money policy was only adopted when there was a balance of payments deficit. Therefore it was easier to achieve the change in relative prices by a rise in both nominal and real wages, and by letting consumer prices rise but keeping wholesale prices stable.

There was also a transitional element involved. When, later, full employment was achieved, and the changes in the distribution of income had run their course, one of the major causes of the relative price change would disappear. If high growth continued with a labour shortage, the

TABLE 2.7 Composition of price indexes, 1970

	Consumer price index % of total	Wholesale price index % of total
Total	100.0	100.0
Goods	67.9	100.0
Industrial goods	46.5	85.5
Products of large co.	22.6	63.3
Products of small/medium co.	23.9	20.1
Non-industrial goods	18.4	14.5
Imported goods	0.0	2.1
Services	32.1	0.0
Breakdown of goods by category		
Consumption goods	100.0	24.5
Production goods	0.0	54.0
Capital goods	0.0	14.1
Export goods	0.0	7.4

Source:
Based on Bank of Japan's Annual Report of Wholesale Price Statistics and Sōrifu Tōkeikyoku (Prime Minister's Office, Statistics Bureau), *Shōhisha Bukka Shisū Nenpō*, 1975.

effect of wage increases would be far more significant. Wholesale prices would inevitably be affected. In fact, as can be seen from Table 2.6, wholesale prices did begin to rise in the late 1960s. They continued to rise gently, until the rapid inflation of 1973–4, which was quite unlike anything experienced during HEGP. This sudden worsening of inflation was caused mainly by three factors:

1. In the 1970s, because of the large balance of payments surplus, the government allowed an enormous increase in the money supply.
2. Demand rose sharply because of Prime Minister Kakuei Tanaka's 'Reorganize the Japanese Archipelago Plans' launched in 1972. (Known as Nihon Rettō Kaizōron, this ambitious plan was to move industries out of Tokyo and spread them throughout the prefectures of Japan. However, its immediate result was a sharp rise in land and other prices, and the over-all plan was eventually rejected. It was, however, welcomed by local governments, many of which continued to implement its ideas.)
3. There was a sharp rise in the price of foreign goods, largely the effect of OPEC's massive increase in oil prices.

Not only was the inflation of 1973–4 much more severe than that of the 1960s, it was also of a completely different nature. First, the increase in wholesale prices was greater than that of consumer prices. Second, there was a sharp rise in the value of assets such as land, stocks, works of art and golf-club membership. The inflation of 1973–4 therefore had the opposite effect on the distribution of income to that of the 1960s. It favoured owners of assets over wage-earners. Furthermore, in contrast to the 1960s it brought about unemployment, because to fight such severe inflation, equally severe monetary measures had to be taken. Such measures brought forth mounting criticism about the social injustices caused by these policies.

2.5 NEW ELEMENTS AFFECTING GROWTH AND THE BUSINESS CYCLE

The investment-led growth of HEGP brought about great changes in the structure of the Japanese economy. Japan's surplus population had made unemployment a perennial problem in the past, but by the late 1960s the ranks of the unemployed had been absorbed. Japanese manufacturers' international competitiveness had improved considerably, raising the balance of payments ceiling.

Until about 1970, due mainly to the increase in gross fixed business capital formation, Japan maintained high growth. Along with high growth went a sharp increase in imports. Because exports were also expanding rapidly, however, there was a continued large trade surplus. The government attempted to reduce this surplus by stimulating internal demand, but it was already at a high level and shortages of labour, land and foreign raw materials upset the plan. The raising of the yen against the dollar (1971) and the changeover to a floating exchange rate (1973) were attempts to deal with this situation. They could not, however, prevent inflation and unemployment becoming the new ceiling and floor for the business cycle. As we will explain in the next chapter, it was because this was not fully realized that there was a serious fall in the growth rate.

APPENDIX 2.1: THE 'TENKEIKI' DEBATE

Between 1955 and 1960 private investment in equipment rose very sharply, much faster in fact than the economic growth rate. In its 1962 annual report, however, the Economic Planning Agency expressed the opinion, based on a model by

Hiroshi Hori,[1] that investment-led growth would not continue, and that the economy was entering a transitional phase (Tenkeiki – literally a period in which the type (of economy) changes) with a new pattern of growth. The discussions on the model and the report centred on three questions.

1. Why had the sharp rise in investment not resulted in supply exceeding demand?
2. Would the level of investment continue to rise?
3. Should investment fall off, would the growth rate be adversely affected?

Here is a condensed version of Hori's model:

For a certain period (in this case 1955–60) Demand, $Y = Y_0 (1 + r)^t$ (Y_0 = demand at the beginning of the period, r = annual growth rate, t = growth over the whole period.)

Capacity, V, will be equal to V_0 (capacity at the beginning of the period) plus accumulated investment for the whole period, $\Sigma_{n=0}^{t} I_n$ (or, with g as the rate of increase in investment, $I_0[(1 + g)^t - 1]/g$) multiplied by k (the reciprocal of the capital coefficient) which expresses the fixed proportion of investment realized in an increase in production. If demand is the same at the beginning and end of the period, we have the following equation:

$$[(1 + g)^t - 1]/g = V_0[(1 + r)^t - 1]/kI_0$$

By using close approximations of actual statistics – $k = 0.8$, $I_0/V_0 = 0.1$ (for 1955), $r = 10\%$ (0.1, for 1955–60), $t = 5$ – Hori got a figure of 0.2 for g.

In 1955–60, therefore, Hori stated, a rate of increase in investment higher than the growth rate had probably been necessary to maintain the balance between supply and demand. However, for the next five-year period, because I_0/V_0 would be about 0.2, even with $r = 0.1$, g would fall to about minus 0.15, so that investment would decrease sharply. (The statistics Hori used were later revised, but this meant only minor changes.) Thus Hori believed that he had conclusively answered questions (1) and (2).

Takao Akabane and others carried out estimates of capital stock, and discovered that in spite of the sharp rise in investment, the increase in capital stock was only about the same as the growth rate.[2] They regarded this as adding support to Hori's view that investment would fall sharply. Miyohei Shinohara accepted Hori's and Akabane's views, and went one step further. He forecast (in answer to question (3)) that the growth rate would also fall.[3]

Most economists accepted Hori's views on supply and demand (question (1)). There was, however, criticism of his forecasts on investment trends. Because k was fixed, the critics said, his model was inflexible, and any forecasts based upon it would be unreliable. There was also disagreement with Shinohara's answer to the third question. It was asserted that the falling-off in equipment investment would be compensated for by demand other than investment.

Looking back, how should we evaluate these discussions? In 1960–5 equipment investment did in fact decrease, showing that Hori's and Shinohara's reasoning had been basically correct. The fall, however, was not as great as the model had predicted, and the economic growth rate, aided by increased government investment and consumption, did not fall. Thus their critics had also been partially correct.[4]

APPENDIX 2.2: PRODUCTIVITY DIFFERENTIAL INFLATION

Yoshihiro Takasuga explained the rise in consumer prices after 1960 as being the result of 'productivity differential inflation'.[5] According to his explanation, there were great differences in the increases in productivity between the various industries. At the same time wages were generally becoming more equal. The lower productivity industries, therefore, confronted with increasing labour costs, had to increase their prices. Because consumer prices were directly affected by the lower productivity areas (e.g. the service and distribution industries) they were pushed up even though wholesale prices remained stable (Tables 2.6, 2.7 and 2.8).

Critics of this view said that while it served to explain the relative price changes, it did not explain the change in absolute prices. It should have been possible, they said, to achieve the same relative price change by a fall in wholesale prices with consumer prices stable. Why, they asked, was this not done? Two common hypotheses are:

1. Because of the considerable increase in the money supply, and in demand.
2. Because the high productivity industries had semi-monopolistic powers, and were able successfully to resist pressures to reduce their prices.[6]

Our opinion, as we explained in the chapter, is that although as (1) says the price rise was the result of an increase in the money supply, this was part of the government policy of maintaining the highest possible growth rate within the limits set by the balance of payments situation. Given that the fixed yen rate had to be maintained, and wholesale prices kept stable, we believe that the productivity differential inflation theory is a tenable explanation for the price changes of the 1960s.

Here we present a model designed to explain our interpretation of productivity differential inflation. Let us imagine an economy with only two industries, and express their respective production functions in a Cobb–Douglas-type model.

$$Q_j = A_j e^{g_j t} K_j^{\alpha j} L_j^{\beta j} \qquad (j = 1, 2)$$

If we find the logarithms of these figures, differentiate them, and express the rate of change in small letters ($q = 1/Q \cdot dQ/dt$) we get:

$$q_j = g_j + \alpha_j k_j + \beta_j l_j \; \text{---} \; (1) \, (2)$$

Next, if we make labour's marginal product equal to its factor price (wages) ($W_j/P_j = Bj Q_j/L_j$), take the logarithms and differentiate them we get:

$$w_j - p_j = q_j - l_j \; \text{---} \; (3) \, (4)$$

If the supply and demand of labour were equal, w_1 would be equal to w_2, but we have to take into account the wage differential, and the fact that it was in the process of narrowing.

$$\therefore \; \text{we get:} \quad \phi w_1 = w_2 \; \text{---} \; (5)$$

With the growth rates for the two industries, q_j, industry no. 1's price rise p_1, its capital savings rate k_1, an exogenous variable, and industry no. 2's capital savings

TABLE 2.8 Inflation indicators, 1973–4

| Calendar year | (1) Consumer prices | % increase or decrease over previous year | | | | (6) Money supply | (7) Ratio of Job offers to job seekers |
		(2) Wholesale prices	(3) Wages (manufacturing industries)	(4) Land prices[a]	(5) Import prices		
1971	Δ 0.8	6.0	13.4	15.7	0.0	24.3	1.12
1972	0.8	4.6	15.6	13.2	Δ 4.3	24.7	1.16
1973	15.8	11.8	14.2	25.1	21.0	16.8	1.76
1974	31.4	24.3	26.0	23.0	66.2	11.5	1.20
1975	3.0	11.9	11.9	Δ 6.9	7.6	14.5	0.61
1976	5.0	9.3	12.6	3.6	6.0	13.5	0.64
1977	1.9	8.1	9.5	2.1	1.5	11.1	0.56
1978	2.5	3.8	6.9	2.8	Δ 16.2	13.1	0.56

Note:
[a] for urban areas throughout Japan.
Source:
Keizai Kikakuchō Chosakyoku (Economic Planning Agency, Research Bureau), *Keizai Yoran*.

rate k_2, we get:

$$k_2 = \theta k_1 \ \text{---} \ (6)$$

Thus there are six equations, and six unknown quantities ($k_2, l_1, l_2, p_2, w_1, w_2$) to be found. With Japan's economy during HEGP in mind, let us now say that industry no. 1 represents manufacturing industries, and industry no. 2 other industries. Using our estimations of the parameters and exogenous variables (Table 2.9) and working out the equations, we get a figure of 5 per cent for p_2, and the other five also work out close to the actual figures for HEGP. Thus, we believe that this model successfully reproduces the productivity differential inflation of HEGP.

Finally, we have to justify the four premises we have assumed.

TABLE 2.9 The mechanism of productivity differential inflation

	α_1	0.3	Author's estimate
	β_1	0.7	Author's estimate
Parameters	α_2	0.2	Author's estimate
	β_2	0.8	Author's estimate
	ϕ	1.2	Approximation
	θ	0.6	Approximation
	q_1	14.9	Increase in the index of manufacturing industries' production
	k_1	13.4	Growth in the capital stock of secondary industries
Exogenous variables	g_1	7.8	Residual (consistent with $\alpha_1 \beta_1 l_1$)
	p_1	1.0	Index in the wholesale price index
	q_2	7.2	Estimated from real GNP and the index of manufacturing industries' production
	g_2	4.8	Residual (consistent with $\alpha_2 \beta_2 l_2$)
	l_1	4.4	Increase in the number of employees in secondary industries (actual figure -4.4%)
Endogenous variables	w_1	9.5	Wage increase for manufacturing companies with 500 or more employees (actual figure -9.7%)
	w_2	11.4	Wage increase for manufacturing companies with 30–99 employees (actual figure -11.0%)
	k_2	8.0	Growth in the capital stock of non-secondary industries (actual figure -8.5%)
	l_2	1.0	Increase in the number of employees in non-secondary industries (actual figure -0.9%)
	p_2	5.2	Increase in consumer prices (actual figure -4.3%)

Note:
Actual figures for endogenous variables are for 1955–70.

1. q_1 and q_2 are exogenous variables. In this model growth is also viewed as an exogenous variable in order to follow up the movements of prices and wages. The effect of these movements on growth is ignored here.

2. $\phi w_1 = w_2$. The supply of labour, and the labour market, are not included in this model. This equation works in their stead. When labour supply is tight, ϕ will rise.

3. k_1 is an exogenous variable. This might appear to be similar to the view that in manufacturing industries investment, priority is given to heavy and chemical industries (as, for example, in the 'Yūshi Shūchū' hypothesis[7]). However, here no such deep meaning is intended, we have merely done this for the sake of convenience, that is, to make the model simpler.

4. p_1 is an exogenous variable. This reflects the fact that (as we explained in the chapter) to maintain the balance of payments, prices of industrial goods for export had to be kept at competitive levels.

Thus, the applications of this model are limited. Calculations on the growth rate, the composition of demand, labour supply, savings, balance of payments, and money supply are outside its confines. However, by using the approximations of HEGP figures with it, we can reproduce the circumstances surrounding the consumer price inflation of that period.

NOTES

1. Hiroshi Hori, 'Tōshi ga Tōshi o yobu Mekanizumu', in Keizai Kikakuchō, Chōsakyoku (Economic Planning Agency, Research Bureau) *Keizai Geppō*, Sept 1961.
2. Keizai Kikakuchō, Keizai Kenkyūjo (Economic Planning Agency, Research Institute) *Shihon Sutokku to Keizai Seichō*, 1962.
3. Miyohei Shinohara, *Nihon Keizai wa Tenkeiki ni aru ka*, Chūōkōron, Keieitokushū, Jan 1962.
4. On whether the 'Tenkeiki' had ended, see Toshio Shishido, 'Tenkeiki wa owatta', *Ekonomisuto*, 17 Jan 1967.
5. Yoshihiro Takasuga, *Gendai Nihon no Bukka Mondai*, new edn, Shinhyōron, 1975, esp. Chapter 1.
6. For information on this hypothesis, see Hiroshi Kawaguchi, 'Nihon no Infureishon – 1960 Nendai ikō no Tenkai o Chūshin ni', in *Gendai Sekai no Infureishon*, compiled by Gendai Infureishon Kenkyūkai, Yūhikaku, 1981.
7. Hiroshi Kawaguchi, 'Shōhisha Bukka Tōki to Yūshi Shūchū Kikō', *Keizai Hyōron*, Dec 1963.

3 From High to Low Growth

3.1 INTRODUCTION

From about 10 per cent during HEGP, the growth rate fell to 4.7 per cent in 1970–5, and 4.9 per cent for 1975–80 (Figure 3.1).

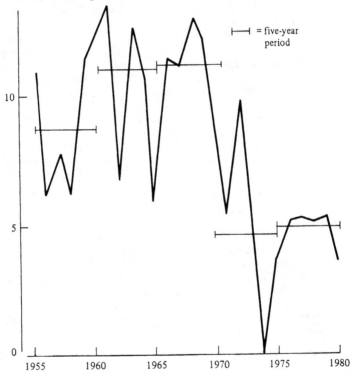

FIGURE 3.1 Fluctuations in the economic growth rate, 1955–80

Sources:
For 1955–65 Keizai Kikakuchō (Economic Planning Agency), *Kokumin Shotoku Tōkei Nenpō*.
For 1965–80 Keizai Kikakuchō (Economic Planning Agency), *Kokumin Keizai Keisan Nenpō*.

In the 1970s the economy was beset by a succession of problems – the appreciation of the yen against the dollar, the oil price rises, high inflation, and recession. It might therefore be argued that short-term problems were largely responsible for the fall in the growth rate. However, it has now been at half that of HEGP for more than ten years, and a return to high growth appears to be out of the question. Therefore we believe we must accept that we have entered a new phase, and that short-term factors are not sufficient to account for the changes that have taken place.

In this chapter we set out the factors responsible for this change, and discuss what adjustments became necessary. Finally, we examine how far we have adjusted.

3.2 THE CAUSES

Why was there a long-term fall in the growth rate after 1970? By dividing Harrod's growth model $GC = s$ (or for our purposes in this chapter, $G_n \times C_r \approx s$) into its three separate elements,[1] we get three possible causes: (i) the effect of the initial fall in the growth rate, (ii) a fall in the efficiency of capital, (iii) a fall in the rate of savings. We consider each of these in turn.

3.2.1 The Natural Rate of Growth

What we can say for certain is that in the 1970s the anticipated long-term growth rate fell significantly (Table 3.1). This can be interpreted in many ways. It could have been simply that seeing the fall in the actual growth rate, people lowered their expectations for the future, and this in turn caused the actual growth rate to fall further. This line of argument, however, could be criticized as simply going round in circles. It might also be argued that the real problem is to find out why the anticipated long-term growth rate fell, and that unless this is known the causes of the fall in the actual growth rate will remain a mystery.

What should be recognized, however, is that a fall in the anticipated growth rate plays a vital part in the 'slowing-down process' of the actual growth rate. Companies' decisions on investment and employment depend largely on the anticipated long-term growth rate, and households' choices on whether to save or consume are governed by 'anticipated long-term income'. To this extent at least, people's expectations have a tendency to be self-realizing.

TABLE 3.1 Company and government forecasts for growth

(a) Company forecasts

Date of survey	Period forecast	Average anticipated growth rate %	Standard deviation %
October 1969	1965–75	10.7	1.7
January 1975	1975–8	5.3	1.8
January 1980	1980–2	5.1	1.0

(b) Government plans

Name of plan	Date formed	Period	Anticipated growth rate %
Keizai Shakai Hatten Keikaku	May 1970	1970–5	10.6
Keizai Shakai Kihon Keikaku	Feb 1973	1973–7	9.4
Shōwa 50 Nendai Zenki Keizai Keikaku	May 1976	1976–80	6
Shinkeizai Shakai 7 Kanen Keikaku	Aug 1979	1979–85	5

Sources:
'Company Forecasts – Survey of Stock-market Listed Companies', in Keizai Kikakuchō (Economic Planning Agency), *Kigyō Kōdō Chōsa* (published annually).

A fall in the anticipated long-term growth rate could be thought of as corresponding to a fall in Harrod's natural rate of growth, G_n. This was originally defined as the rate of growth permitted by the increase in population, and technical progress.[2] Within this definition G_n appears to be purely objective, that is to say, it excludes subjective elements such as people's expectations. In actual fact, however, an increase in population cannot simply be converted into an increase in labour supply, because labour supply is affected by people's choices about hours of leisure. In fact, whether it be in judgements on the future availability of raw materials, or about the quality of the environment, people's judgement is always involved to some extent. Thought of in this way, the natural rate of growth clearly includes a subjective element. The factors that bear on the future natural growth rate – choice of leisure hours, technical change, availability of raw materials – can only be estimated, not measured accurately. Therefore, assuming that the process by which people's expectations are formed is rational, the anticipated long-term growth rate will be equal to the natural growth rate. Or, if we cannot go as far as to say this, we could say that because the natural growth rate cannot be measured *ex ante*, the anticipated growth rate serves the same function in real life which the natural growth rate serves in models.

Bearing in mind the anticipated growth rate's vital role in the growth process, let us now consider why it fell. Inevitably, this must of course be to some extent guesswork, but the following reasons are all tenable:

1. The supply of raw materials and energy, shortages of suitable land for industry, and growing concern over pollution of the environment were increasingly checking growth.
2. There was a fall-off in the supply of labour.
3. Technical progress began to slow down as Japan caught up with other advanced industrial nations.
4. The expansion of exports slowed down as Japan's increasing share of the world market began to create friction.
5. There was a change in people's sense of values regarding economic growth. They began to want more leisure and became more concerned about improving the environment, while many companies, worried by an uncertain future, aimed for stability rather than high growth.

It is, however, difficult to determine how much each of these elements affected the anticipated growth rate. Furthermore, the situation was changing constantly during the 1970s. A piece of research in the mid-1970s suggested that with a possible increase in the supply of 'primary energy' for 1975–80 of 6.3 per cent, assuming that the elasticity of GNP relative to energy consumption fell from 1.2 in the past, to 0.95, the maximum possible growth rate was 6.6 per cent.[3] However, with progress in energy conservation, the elasticity of GNP relative to energy consumption fell sharply, to 0.65 for 1975–9, so that a much higher growth rate was actually possible.

However, there were also people who thought that because of the instability of energy supply and prices it was wise to calculate on the safe side, so that to them a lower rate of growth was acceptable.

In other words, what kept the growth rate down was not so much the physical limits of the availability of raw materials, but rather the uncertainty involved, which made forecasting the future such a difficult task.

3.2.2 The Rise in the Capital Coefficient

As can be seen from Table 3.2, during the 1970s the marginal capital coefficient rose from its HEGP level of 1.5 to over 3. As will be explained

TABLE 3.2 Changes in the capital coefficient, 1965–8

	1965–70	1970–5	1975–80
Economic growth Rate A	11.2%	4.7%	4.9%
Gross fixed capital formation B	31.3%	34.4%	32.3%
Private investment in plant and equipment C	16.7%	17.6%	16.0%
Marginal capital coefficient $\dfrac{B}{A}$	2.79	7.32	6.59
Marginal capital coefficient $\dfrac{C}{A}$	1.49 ·	3.72	3.26
Average capital coefficent	1.04	1.37	1.46

Source:
Keizai Kikakuchō (Economic Planning Agency) *Kokumin Keizai Keisan Nenpō*, 1982.

later, when the natural growth rate was falling rapidly the rise in the required capital coefficient may actually have helped to stabilize the economy. In the long term, however, it acted as an obstacle to a return to high growth.

The question we must answer here is how much of the rise in the capital coefficient was the result of required capital coefficient, and how much it was caused by the fall in the growth rate. A fall in the growth rate automatically brings about a rise in the capital coefficient. Capital coefficient $= I/\Delta Y$. When the growth rate falls, replacement investment's share of gross plant and equipment investment increases. When this happens, the numerator I rises steadily, but the denominator ΔY is not affected, so the capital coefficient rises. Let us illustrate this by looking at the period 1970–80. The ratio of replacement investment to GNP was 5.3 per cent in 1970, and 6.6 per cent in 1980 (Table 3.3) while the ratio of new investment fell from 14.3 per cent in 1970 to 10.2 per cent in 1980. As a proportion of gross investment, replacement investment rose from 27 per cent in 1970 to 39 per cent in 1980. This explains why even though the growth rate fell sharply in the 1970s, plant and equipment investment remained relatively unchanged. Although the ratio of new investment fell by about 40 per cent (from 14.3 to 10.2), the over-all investment ratio actually rose slightly.

The fall in the growth rate also caused the capital coefficient to rise:

(a) because it was caused by a slowing down in the rate of technical progress;

TABLE 3.3 Replacement investment, the capital coefficient, and the increase in the capital stock

1970–80

	Investment ratio (1) %	Average capital coefficient (2) %	Depreciation (3) %	Replacement investment ratio ((2) × (3)) (4) %	New investment ratio ((1) − (4)) (5) %	Rate of increase in capital stock (≈ (5) − (2)) (6) %
1970	19.6	1.04	5.11	5.3	14.3	14.4
1975	16.4	1.37	4.43	6.1	10.3	7.5
1980	16.8	1.46	4.52	6.6	10.2	6.6

Source:
Keizai Kikakuchō (Economic Planning Agency), *Sōgō Keikaku Kyoku Shiryō*, July 1981.

(b) because there was a fall in real interest rates. Thus the rise in the capital coefficient was at least to some extent the result of the falling growth rate.

We must also take into consideration certain other factors that raised the required capital coefficient. Here we are referring to the increasing proportion of investment in energy conservation projects, automation and other labour-saving projects, preservation of the environment, and in building up stocks of raw materials. The rise in the required capital coefficient was a combination of the effects of a falling growth rate and of these factors.

A look at the performance of different industries in the 1970s reveals that in the mid-1970s, when the working ratio of capital was falling, there was a significant rise in the average capital coefficient, and that also in the late 1970s the trend was upward for most industries (Table 3.4). In the wholesale and retail trades, and electricity and gas, the capital coefficient rose considerably. In the manufacturing sector, however, the rise was not as great, and in industries where technical progress was still marked, the capital coefficient actually fell. Thus the change in the emphasis on equipment investment from the manufacturing to the non-manufacturing sector was another factor in the rise of the capital coefficient.

3.2.3 The Rate of Savings

Finally, let us examine the effect of the fall in the rate of savings. The proportion of savings that can be exploited domestically is affected by changes in the terms of trade. The rises in the price of imported oil adversely affected the terms of trade, and this in turn reduced the proportion of savings that could be used within Japan. After a period when the nominal current account was balanced, export prices remained unchanged, but the price of oil imports rose sharply. A current account balance was later achieved once more, which implies that either exports had increased sharply or imports had fallen sharply. In either case it meant a large balance of payments surplus in real terms. This surplus corresponded to the shift in income to the oil-producing countries, and it meant that this amount of savings could not be used for domestic capital formation.

If we call this real surplus b, the growth model now becomes $GC = s - b$.[4] The value of b depends on the scale of the inflow of capital. In Japan the nominal current account was virtually balanced, while the

TABLE 3.4 Changes in the capital coefficient in different industries, 1970–9

	Over-all capital coefficient	Manufacturing industries						Non-manufacturing		
		Average for manufacturing sector	Textiles	Chemicals	Metals	Electrical products	Motor vehicles	Wholesale and retail trades	Electricity and gas	Service industry
1970	1.08	1.48	2.15	3.18	2.78	1.36	1.12	4.51	1.47	0.38
1971	1.16	1.61	2.36	2.95	2.82	1.40	1.31	4.46	1.54	0.42
1972	1.17	1.65	2.61	2.27	2.80	1.14	1.42	4.90	1.66	0.45
1973	1.19	1.61	2.68	2.88	2.71	0.96	1.35	5.51	1.65	0.51
1974	1.33	1.78	2.34	3.06	3.26	1.04	1.34	6.16	1.68	0.60
1975	1.42	2.00	2.59	3.45	3.43	1.25	1.50	6.17	1.76	0.67
1976	1.44	1.86	2.52	3.25	3.18	0.94	1.40	6.54	1.81	0.74
1977	1.46	1.83	2.38	2.82	3.46	0.88	1.33	7.48	1.96	0.78
1978	1.47	1.78	2.51	2.40	3.45	0.78	1.34	7.46	2.12	0.86
1979	1.47	1.70	2.40	2.52	2.91	0.68	1.34	7.34	2.21	0.88

Source:
Keizai Kikakuchō (Economic Planning Agency), *Sōgō Keikaku Kyoku Shiryō*, July 1981.

balance in real terms (at 1975 prices) rose from minus 1.5 per cent of GNP in the first half of the 1970s to plus 2.2 per cent in the second half (Table 3.5). A change in the distribution of income is another factor that can affect the rate of savings. If the relative share of profits falls and the relative share of wages rises, a fall in the propensity to save ensues, pushing down the rate of savings. (see Table 3.6). However, what actually happened was: (i) labour's share of income rose sharply in the mid-1970s, but remained steady in the late 1970s, (ii) company profits and savings did fall in the mid-1970s but, as if to offset this, there was a sharp rise in personal savings. In other words, there seems to have been, at least to some extent, a substitutional relationship between company savings and personal savings.[5]

In the 1970s, despite the oil price rises, Japan managed to balance its nominal current account, though the government's budget deficit increased. Prices gradually stabilized, and interest rates fell. From all this it is difficult to put forward lack of savings as a major factor in the fall of the growth rate. We would suggest rather that the fall in the anticipated long-term growth rate and the slow-down in capital investment it led to were more significant.

TABLE 3.5 Terms of trade and foreign trade balance, 1970–80

	Terms of trade 1975 = 100	Nominal foreign trade balance (% of GNP)	Real foreign trade balance (% of GNP)
1970	139.4	1.2	−2.5
1971	141.9	2.7	−1.1
1972	142.1	2.0	−1.8
1973	124.3	−0.9	−3.8
1974	105.7	−0.4	−1.2
1975	98.2	0.1	0.3
1976	94.2	0.9	1.8
1977	97.2	1.9	2.7
1978	106.1	1.3	0.8
1979	83.8	−1.3	1.3
1980	73.2	−0.5	4.4

Source:
Keizai Kikakuchō (Economic Planning Agency), *Kokumin Keizai Keisan Nenpō*, 1982.

TABLE 3.6 Changes in savings and the distribution of income, 1965–80

	1965	1970	1975	1980
$\dfrac{\text{Income of persons employed}}{\text{National income}}$	55.3	53.6	66.5	67.4
$\dfrac{\text{Company income}}{\text{National income}}$	10.7	17.4	7.6	9.7
$\dfrac{\text{Personal savings}}{\text{Personal disposable income}}$	15.5	18.6	22.2	19.5
$\dfrac{\text{Company savings}}{\text{Company income}}$	—	45.7	19.0	4.1

Source:
Keizai Kikakuchō (Economic Planning Agency), *Kokumin Keizai Keisan Nenpō*, 1982.

3.3 PROBLEMS OF ADJUSTMENT

3.3.1 The Natural Growth Rate and the Warranted Growth Rate

After the first oil price rise, the fall in the anticipated and actual growth rates had a great impact on the economy, necessitating a considerable amount of adjustment.[6]

As was said in the previous section, the natural growth rate fell significantly in the 1970s. During the traumatic period 1973–5, however, the fall in the actual growth rate was even greater. The warranted growth rate appears to have actually risen during this period (Table 3.2). This situation ($G < G_n < G_w$) proved to be a major dilemma in the adjustment period that followed HEGP (see Figure 3.2)

The warranted growth rate can be found by dividing the rate of savings by the required capital coefficient ($G_w = s/C_r$). In other words, G_w is the growth rate when *ex ante* investment is equal to *ex ante* savings. When this is the case, the satisfaction of the business world can be guaranteed. If, however, the actual growth rate is less than the warranted growth rate, even if the economy is expanding there will be no general feeling of satisfaction and prosperity. Even after the economy had recovered from the minus and zero growth of the post-oil price rise period, the feeling of depression remained for a long time. This was because the actual growth rate remained below the warranted growth rate.

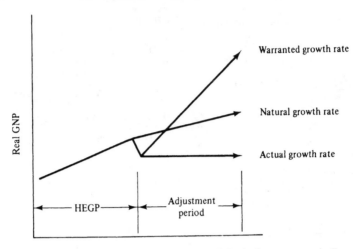

FIGURE 3.2 The economic dilemma of the 'adjustment period'

What actually happens when G is lower than G_w? The amount by which *ex ante* savings are greater than investment may perhaps be offset by (i) a fall in company savings, (ii) a fall in government savings, (iii) an international balance of payments (current account) surplus, or (iv) the actual capital coefficient may be greater than the required capital coefficient, so that the balance will be restored *post ante*. This situation could be brought about by a fall in the working ratio of capital and cumulative stockpiling.

These four things all actually took place during the long recession of 1974–8 (Table 3.7).

Also, when G was lower than G_w, the following factors worked to widen the gap further (i.e. they pushed G down further). Companies, faced with losses, excess stocks, and a falling working ratio of capital, tried to reduce production even further, but this served only to spread the recession. Fears of a tax increase grew as the government deficit rose. This deficit also reduced the extent to which the government could act to relieve the situation. The continuing balance of payments surplus increased friction with other countries, and this caused further uncertainty.

Finally, what made matters even worse was that the fall in G brought about a fall in the natural growth rate, G_n. In the mid-1970s the personal savings rate rose, pushing up G_w, and further aggravating the problem. The rise in personal savings was the result of the fall in the anticipated

TABLE 3.7 Indicators of imbalance during the 'adjustment period', 1973–9

	Ratio of net current profits (before tax) to sales, for corporate business	Balance of payments (current account)	Index of operating ratio of manufacturing industries	Index of inventory/ sales ratio of manufacturing industries	Unemployment %
1973	3.8	Δ 136	128.1	64.0	1.4
1974	2.2	Δ 4 693	117.3	88.5	1.3
1975	1.3	Δ 682	100.0	100.0	1.4
1976	2.1	3 680	108.3	89.0	1.9
1977	2.1	10 918	107.5	90.2	2.0
1978	2.6	16 534	110.7	84.3	2.2
1979	3.0	Δ 8 643	118.9	77.4	2.1

Source:
Keizai Kikakuchō (Economic Planning Agency), Keizai Yōran, 1981.

long-term growth rate and the fall in the proportion of guaranteed long-term income. If just G had been low, and G_n and G_w had been equal, it would have been possible to increase the actual growth rate by stimulating demand. However, if G_n is less than G_w, as it is physically impossible for G to exceed G_n, G is necessarily lower than G_w. Thus when a long-term fall in the growth rate is anticipated, short-term government measures to stimulate demand tend to have little effect. During the long mid-1970s recession the government increased its expenditure on investment in an effort to bring about a recovery. Private companies, however, feared that if government expenditure on investment was increased at the beginning of the year it would in all probability be reduced later in the year. In its economic plan for 1975–80, the government declared that it was aiming for higher growth in the earlier part of the planned period. This was construed as meaning that in the latter part of the period the growth rate would again fall. Faced with this attitude, short-term measures to expand demand had little or no effect, and the recession continued.

Thus during this period, the $G < G_n < G_w$ dilemma greatly perplexed economists. For example, Hisao Kanamori maintained that because the rate of savings was still high a return to high growth was possible, but he was talking mainly about G_w.[7] Osamu Shimomura forecast that because of oil supply problems the growth rate would fall to zero; he was looking at the problem from the point of view of G_n.[8] Because these two leading figures were looking at different aspects of the problem discussions between them were inconclusive, for they were of course talking at cross purposes.

3.3.2 The Coexistence of Inflation and Unemployment

What made adjustment to low growth much more difficult were the measures adopted to control inflation, but these measures were most certainly necessary. In 1974–5, because prices were still rising fast, there was a large drop in production and employment levels.

From Table 3.8 we can compare the changes in money supply, prices and production in 1974 with those of previous recessions. Despite the very tight monetary policies of 1974, pressure from rising prices was still great, so that production was depressed. This fall in production brought about a much greater drop in employment than in previous recessions (Table 3.9).

Another factor involved was that Japan's lifetime employment system makes it very difficult to make regular employees redundant. Employment is Japanese companies' longest-term form of fixed investment. Thus, when the anticipated growth rate fell they had to exercise

TABLE 3.8 Movements of money, prices and production

	Money supply	Velocity of circulation	Wholesale prices	Industrial production
3rd cycle (1958)	1.016	0.834	0.927	0.914
4th cycle (1962)	1.183	0.834	0.979	1.008
5th cycle (1965)	1.184	0.868	1.008	1.018
6th cycle (1971)	1.402	0.732	0.992	1.034
7th cycle (1974)	1.152	0.862	1.305	0.761

Note:
The rate of change is from the trough of each cycle to its peak. For the seventh cycle, the rate of change is from the October–December period of 1973 to the January–March period of 1975.
Source:
Keizai Kikakuchō (Economic Planning Agency), *Keiki Hendō Kansoku Shiryō Nenpō*, 1981.

TABLE 3.9 Changes in production and employment, 1958–74

	Non-scheduled working hours (manufacturing industries)	Regular employment (all industries)	New job offers (excluding new graduates)	Operating ratio (manufacturing industries)	Output of capital goods (excluding motor vehicles)
3rd cycle (1958)	Δ 18.1	5.8	Δ 3.0	Δ 19.9	Δ 15.4
4th cycle (1962)	Δ 22.1	6.0	Δ 4.4	Δ 10.1	Δ 10.4
5th cycle (1965)	Δ 17.0	2.7	Δ 22.9	Δ 7.6	Δ 0.8
6th cycle (1971)	Δ 21.9	2.2	Δ 16.1	Δ 6.7	Δ 8.0
7th cycle (1974)	Δ 38.3·	Δ 0.4	Δ 42.7	Δ 15.7	Δ 10.2

Note:
The rate of exchange is from the trough of each cycle to its peak.

extreme caution in deciding the number of new regular employees they could take on. The fall in the anticipated growth rate was therefore strongly reflected in the employment figures. (The number of new regular employees continued to fall after 1974.)

When the modern economy was hit by both inflation and unemployment it proved to be surprisingly fragile. During HEGP the idea of a 'Taishū Shōhi Shakai', that is, that the public was like a marionette and that merely by 'pulling the strings' it could be made to increase consumption at any time, was widely accepted. Thus it was believed that a recession could be stopped in its tracks at any time, merely by stimulating personal consumption. Faced with both inflation and unemployment, however, households lost confidence in the future, and so reduced their consumption, increased savings and invested less in housing (Table 3.10). Thus the 'Taishū Shōhi Shakai' myth was destroyed.

It had also come to be believed during HEGP that demand could be regulated by a flexible fiscal policy and that a recession could quickly be brought under control. When, however, inflation and recession existed side by side, this was no longer feasible, because a tight money policy had to be adopted to combat inflation. Continuing inflation after the budget had been announced caused a fall in real government expenditure, but any attempt at positive measures to fight the recession would have meant

TABLE 3.10 Demand fluctuation during recession periods, 1958–74

	Personal consumption expenditure	Private housing construction	Government current expenditure	Government fixed capital formation	Private inventory investment	Corporate equipment investment	GNP
3rd cycle (1958)	8.0	12.4	5.1	25.4	Δ87.3	Δ10.2	5.0
4th cycle (1962)	9.5	12.8	9.0	28.4	—	Δ 2.5	3.6
5th cycle (1965)	4.7	15.1	6.8	18.7	Δ34.8	Δ12.9	4.1
6th cycle (1971)	9.5	8.7	11.3	36.6	Δ20.5	1.6	10.8
7th cycle (1974)	3.5	Δ17.6	7.5	9.3	Δ58.6	Δ24.8	Δ8.5

Note:
The rate of change is from the trough of each cycle to its peak.
Source:
Keizai Kikakuchō (Economic Planning Agency), *Kokumin Shotoku Keisan*, Nenpō, 1977 (in real terms).

a huge government deficit. Also, with the anticipated growth rate falling, the government doubted whether it could make up such a deficit in the future by increasing taxes.

Thus faith in the government's ability to maintain full employment by regulating demand (which had generally been believed possible during HEGP) was shaken. This loss of confidence resulted in the much deeper recession of the mid-1970s.

3.3.3 The End of the Tunnel

The nation gradually adjusted to the new situation, and as time went by things began to improve. The personal savings rate, which had for a time risen sharply with the fall in the anticipated growth rate, gradually came down as actual growth settled down at a lower rate. The capital coefficient rose, while interest rates fell and the repayment of fixed costs progressed. As a result of all this, the gap between G and G_w shrank, as G_w fell. Companies were able to operate at a profit in spite of low growth, and with increased unemployment labour unions' wage demands were becoming lower. The anticipated rate of inflation was also falling, and from the second half of 1977 the government, forseeing a period in which the fear of inflation would no longer unduly restrict expansionist policies, began taking positive measures to stimulate demand.

At the end of 1978, just before OPEC's second major price rise, prices were more stable than they had been since 1960 and the balance of payments situation was stable and healthy. Unemployment was higher than it had been before the first oil price rise, but it was not increasing. Company profits were of course lower than during HEGP, but compared with immediately after the first oil price rise when many companies had operated at a loss, the situation had improved greatly. The difference between the anticipated long-term growth rate, the rate of increase in the stock of capital, and the actual growth rate, had lessened. Leaving aside the problem of a still-large government deficit, we think we can say that by the late 1970s the economy had more or less adjusted to the new conditions.

3.4 A NEW PHASE OF GROWTH

At the end of the 1970s the economy entered a new phase. The anticipated annual long-term growth rate is now 4–5 per cent and the stock of capital is increasing at about 6 per cent. This figure has been achieved because 15–16 per cent of GNE is going into plant and equipment investment. Assuming that the average capital coefficient continues its present rate of increase, and a growth rate of around 5 per cent is achieved, this level of increase in capital stock (capacity) is likely to continue. Looked at in this way, capacity seems to be increasing in proportion to the anticipated growth rate, and it looks as though a steady growth can be achieved. It is still too early to forecast this with confidence, however, because of unknown factors such as future energy prices and the rate of technological change.

The actual growth rate for 1980–1 was lower than the above-mentioned anticipated growth rate, largely because of the 1979 oil price rise and the monetary measures that had to be taken. Even leaving aside such short-term factors, however, we think that for the following reasons a middle- or long-term fall in demand is likely:

1. A possible slowing-down of exports. As the world-wide recession drags on, resentment over Japan's increasing exports is growing.
2. There is a possibility that government expenditure will be reduced. Since the first oil price rise the Treasury has built up an enormous debt. In order to reduce it, sweeping reforms of government procedure are planned and it is also feared that there will be tax increases. However, some economists believe that even if government expenditure is reduced it will not cause deflation, because (i) crowding out on the capital market will cease and private investment will increase, (ii) private savings will fall as government savings increase. Also, if the productivity of the (e.g. national railways) public sector improves, it could, in the long term, bring about an increase in the over-all productivity of the economy. In actual fact, however, a reduction in government expenditure would, through the multiplier effect, cause a fall-off in the increase in demand. Crowding out has not really been marked anyway, and there does not seem to be such a close substitutional relationship between personal and government savings.[9] Therefore during the 'rebuilding of government finances' we can expect a reduction of the increase in demand.
3. The effects of population changes. The post-war bulge generation have now found work and got married. Because of this the tempo of the movement to the cities has slowed down and demand for consumer durables and housing appears to be reaching its limits. Also, because the population is ageing fast, fears of not having enough to live on in old age have increased the propensity to save and invest. These developments reduce consumption and increase resistance to falling interest rates, thereby slowing demand.

Finally, we should bear in mind that adjustment to the new oil prices is still continuing, and that some industries are still suffering from structural recession. Thus it is uncertain whether or not the anticipated growth rate can be achieved. However, the personal savings rate is still high, people's will to work still strong, and industry has not lost its dynamism, so we believe that provided government finances can be successfully 'rebuilt', a growth rate of 4–5 per cent is possible.

NOTES

1. R. F. Harrod, *Towards a Dynamic Economics*, Macmillan, 1956.
2. Ibid, p. 87.
3. Keizai Shingikai (Economic Council), 'Shōwa 50 Nendai no Senzai Seichōryoku to Kongo no Mondaiten', in Keizai Kikakuchō (Economic Planning Agency), *Atarashii Keizai Kikaku*, 1976.
4. Harrod, *Towards a Dynamic Economics*, p. 105.
5. The substitutional relationship between personal and company savings was found by Denison to exist in the USA, and is now included in theories on savings there (e.g. von Furstenberg). (See E. Denison, 'A Note on Private

TABLE 3.11 The relationship between personal savings, company savings and government savings in Japan, the USA, West Germany, the UK, and Sweden

	National disposable income b	Corporate savings c	Government savings d	R^2
Japan (1967–79)	0.18(23.00)	Δ0.80(Δ4.26)	Δ0.07(Δ0.36)	0.99
USA (1967–78)	0.04 (6.05)	Δ0.66(Δ3.07)	Δ0.22(Δ1.94)	0.88
West Germany (1967–78)	0.10(11.71)	Δ0.60(Δ2.28)	Δ0.08(Δ0.67)	0.95
UK (1967–78)	0.09(11.50)	Δ0.19(Δ1.90)	Δ0.40(Δ2.82)	0.99
Sweden (1967–78)	0.09 (9.90)	Δ0.14(Δ1.04)	Δ0.29(Δ2.48)	0.98

Note:
Figures in brackets = *t*-value.
Sources:
Japan – Keizai Kikakuchō (Economic Planning Agency), *Kokumin Keizai Keisan Nenpō*, 1981.
Other countries – Yutaka Kosai's calculations from *UN Yearbook of National Accounts*, 1979.

TABLE 3.12 A breakdown of the causes of the fall in the growth rate

	1965-73	1974-9	The difference
Gross domestic product	9.4	4.9	−4.5
Capital's contribution	3.3	1.9	−1.4
Labour's contribution	0.4	1.0	+0.6
The contribution of energy price changes	0.3	−1.8	−2.1
The contribution of capital's age	0.7	−0.8	−1.5
Technical progress's contribution	4.6	4.6	0

Saving', *Review of Economics and Statistics*, Aug 1958; G. M. von Furstenberg, 'Private Saving', *American Economic Review*, May 1980.) In Japan it did not apparently exist in the 1960s (Ishikawa) and was first recognized in the 1970s (Kōsai). (See Tsuneo Ishikawa, 'Chochiku no Shokeitai ni kansuru – Kōsatsu – Kojin Chochiku to Seido Chochiku no Kankei', in Nihon Ginkō Chochiku Suishinkyoku's *Chochiku Jihō*, no. 118; Yutaka Kōsai, 'Kojin Chochiku to sono ta Chochiku no Kankei – sono saikin no Keikō', in Nihon Ginkō Chochiku Suishinkyoku's *Chochiku Jihō*, no. 127.

Using the regression formula, $S_H = a + bY + cS_B + dS_G$ (S_H = personal savings, Y = national disposable income, S_B = company savings, S_q = government savings) the following figures were obtained for the relationship between the various branches of savings for Japan and four other countries (Table 3.11).

According to these calculations, in Japan, the USA and West Germany, 60–80 per cent of company savings can be substituted for by personal savings.

6. Some economists believe that the oil price rise was directly responsible for the fall in productivity. Further research is necessary on this question, but according to the Economic Planning Agency's calculations (Table 3.12) of the 5 per cent fall in the growth rate, the first oil price rise was responsible for 2 per cent, while the fall-off in capital savings (including ageing of capital stock) accounted for 3 per cent. The calculations on the contribution of energy price changes used the method presented in R. H. Rasche and J. A. Tatom, 'Energy Resources and Potential GNP', *Review of the Federal Reserve Bank of St Louis*, June 1977.

7. Hisao Kanamori, *Nihon Keizai Kōgi*, Nihon Keizai Shinbunsha, 1979, esp. pp. 236–60.

8. Osamu Shimomura and Yukio Suzuki, *Teiseichō o dō ikiru*, Zaikei Shōhōsha, 1978.

9. As can be seen from Table 3.11, there is apparently no substitutional relationship between personal savings and government savings in Japan.

4 Industrial Structure and Organization

4.1 INTRODUCTION

If we compare Japan with other leading industrial nations we find that the proportion of primary industries is rather high (though lower than France), the proportion of secondary industries is about average (lower than West Germany), while the proportion of tertiary industries is about the same as in most Western European countries, but lower than in the USA and the UK. A comparison of manufacturing industries reveals that in Japan the proportion of heavy industries and chemical industries is very high (Table 4.1). The present industrial structure is largely the result of a sharp fall in the proportion of primary industries, and a corresponding rise in that of secondary and tertiary industries during HEGP. During the 1970s the proportion of secondary industries fell slightly and that of tertiary industries rose.

The theme of this chapter is the industrialization process, and an evaluation of the present situation. In section 4.2 we look at the factors that brought about industrialization, particularly the development of heavy and chemical industries. In Japan it is widely believed that these industries were built up in defiance of, rather than in response to, market forces, by deliberate government policy. We examine this hypothesis, and the criticism of its defects, in detail. In section 4.3 we look at how these industries in particular have sought after large-scale production, and discuss (i) whether or not this led to a reduction of competition and a concomitant role of monopoly power, (ii) finding this not to be the case, we examine the factors that prevented it. Finally, we take a look at what is considered to be one of the special characteristics of Japan's industrial organization, the subcontracting system.

TABLE 4.1 A comparison of the industrial structure of Japan, the USA, the UK, France, and West Germany (% value added)

	Japan 1960	Japan 1965	Japan 1970	Japan 1975	USA 1967	UK 1968	France 1965	West Germany 1970
Primary industries	12.55	9.27	6.07	5.16	3.06	2.43	8.08	3.25
Secondary industries	43.48	43.31	46.18	40.59	39.90	44.87	45.44	55.35
Mining	3.18	2.86	2.58	0.52	2.56	2.28	1.97	3.22
Manufacturing	31.52	30.39	32.99	28.33	29.32	31.82	31.38	40.75
heavy/chemical	17.09	17.41	20.62	18.83	17.18	18.23	16.81	23.02
	(54.22)	(56.40)	(62.50)	(66.47)	(56.59)	(57.27)	(53.57)	(56.49)
light industries	14.43	13.25	12.37	9.49	12.14	13.60	14.57	17.73
Construction	6.24	7.39	8.26	9.57	5.79	7.21	9.79	8.73
Electricity and gas	2.54	2.67	2.35	2.17	2.23	3.56	2.30	2.65
Tertiary industries	43.98	47.42	47.74	54.25	57.02	52.70	46.49	41.40
Commerce	12.16	13.21	13.74	14.13	15.05	11.57	14.70	11.55
Transport/communication	7.43	7.69	6.99	6.08	6.14	8.11	4.86	6.54
Services	13.90	15.77	18.98 }	34.04	24.37	16.34	18.16	14.07
Public services	10.49	10.75	8.03 }		11.46	16.67	8.97	9.24

Note:
The figures in brackets are heavy and chemical industries as a ratio of manufacturing industries.
Sources:
Input–output tables for the respective countries.
74 nendo Keizai Hakusho for Japan 1960, 1965, 1970 with figures for 1975 added.

4.2 INDUSTRIALIZATION AND CHANGES IN THE INDUSTRIAL STRUCTURE

4.2.1 Industrialization before the Second World War

Although this book is about the contemporary Japanese economy, a look at the pre-war period is necessary to understand recent industrial development and the various theories on it.

Before the Second World War, Japan exported light industrial goods (e.g. cotton fabrics) to China, India, and other Asian countries, while she imported raw materials from these areas, and machinery from the USA and Europe. This triangular trade stemmed from these areas' relative factor endowment. Japan had abundant labour, Europe and the USA had the capital, and Asia had raw materials. In other words, this trade could be explained by the theory of comparative cost.

There is, however, another conflicting view of Japan's industrialization. It says that after the Meiji Restoration (1868) the government adopted a policy of promoting certain industries in defiance of market forces as part of their plans to make Japan a powerful economic and military nation. (The slogan in those days was 'Fukoku Kyōhei', literally wealthy country, strong army.) This is probably the most commonly accepted theory in Japan. It makes the mistake, however, of equating what actually happened with the government's plans – in other words, of overestimating their success.

By the terms of the treaty signed when Japan reopened the country for foreign trade, the government forfeited the right to fix tariffs, and was therefore unable to indulge in protectionism. It did attempt to foster heavy industry, for example by establishing a national iron works, but like England in the nineteenth century textiles continued to be the main industry. The government's efforts were not very successful, and the industrial development that did take place was the result of market forces. The government's greatest achievements in this period were public undertakings such as improvements in education and the legal system, and in building up the infrastructure of the economy.

This debate has been continuing for a very long time.[1] The opposing theories of post-HEGP industrial development are in fact an extension of it.

*4.2.2 Japan's Present Industrial Structure and the Theory of
Comparative cost*

In one respect at least, the pre-war industrial pattern did not change after the war. Japan still imports raw materials and exports manufactured products. Because she has abundant labour but limited natural resources, this could be said to be her destiny.

The problem for the post-war economy was, which manufacturing industries should be developed? The ones that developed most were in fact heavy and chemical industries. Can this also be explained by the theory of comparative cost? A famous economist and former high official in MITI (the Ministry of International Trade and Industry), Naohiro Amaya, answered this question in the negative.[2] He said that post-war Japan had none of the factors of production – capital, land, raw materials – necessary to promote the growth of heavy and chemical industries. The only factor of production Japan had in abundance, he said, was labour, and that if Japan was to follow the comparative cost theory, the logical answer was to concentrate on labour-intensive light industries such as textiles. Thus Japan's post-war development, he said, could not be explained by orthodox economic theory – that is, as being simply the result of market forces. This development, he said, was the result of deliberate government policy. This view is shared by a great number of people.

We believe, however, that this interpretation of factor endowment is far too narrow and inflexible. In other words, it is not merely a question of amounts, but also of quality. (Just as in Chapter 1, in the section on growth accounting, we said that when measuring factor inputs we also had to include improvements in quality.) Labour, for example, is not simply a question of counting heads. We must also take into account levels of education, training and dedication. In the pre-war textile industry, the majority of employees were young female workers, and their average length of service was extremely short. In contrast, the majority of workers in the heavy and chemical industries of HEGP were skilled, lifetime employees with at least twelve years of education. Thus, in terms of quality, they were vastly superior. The abundance of skilled labour was a particularly important source of comparative advantage for the heavy industries in general, and the machinery industries in particular.

Japan is not only short of raw materials. For geographical reasons the amount of land suitable for industry is also limited. There is, however, one factor that makes the land available very advantageous for heavy industry. This is the abundance of harbours and coastal areas suitable for industry. As marine transport improved and its cost fell,[3] industries on the coast were able to obtain raw materials and export finished products much more cheaply than those inland. Thus Japan's long coastline was a great advantage.

The same can be said about capital. It is not simply a question of the amount of capital stock. Depending on when equipment was made and installed, the technological level is different. Thus the age of capital stock is more important than the actual amount. Thanks to a high rate of savings and a constant supply of new capital equipment, Japan's heavy and chemical industries' capital stock was on average very young, thus giving it a comparative advantage.

Like any other theory, the comparative cost theory should not be regarded as unchangeable. We must be prepared to amend it and make it more sophisticated as the occasion demands. The training of labour and the development of the coastal regions was a long process, and during this time technology was of course advancing. Thus, with these factors, changes in the international situation, and improvements in the infrastructure, factor endowment was continually changing.

Japan's comparative advantage has in fact changed considerably with the passage of time. Hisao Kanamori's comparative study of labour productivity in the UK and Japan in 1955 showed that productivity was higher in Japan in the cotton, rayon, and cement industries, but lower in the steel-plating, chemicals, and machinery industries (Table 4.2). In 1977 (according to the Rōdōshō's (Ministry of Labour) *Rōdō Hakusho*) labour productivity was higher in Japan than in the USA in the following industries: motor vehicles, general machinery, ceramics, and steel; while it was lower in foodstuffs, clothing, chemicals, non-metal products, oil products, precision instruments and textiles (Table 4.3). While labour productivity is only a part of total production costs, it gives us some idea of general trends.

Next let us take a look at the products traded between the USA and Japan. In 1965 Japan's most important exports were steel and textiles; in 1975 they were cars, steel, and household electric appliances. Machinery (especially advanced-technology products such as aircraft and calculators) was the USA's main export in both years, but while soybeans were the next most important in 1966, in 1975 coal and timber were more important and cotton had lost a lot of ground (Table 4.4). Both had abundant factors of production – the USA had land, and research and development, and Japan had 'young' equipment and skilled, disciplined labour.

62

TABLE 4.2 A comparison of labour productivity in Japan and the UK
$$\left(\frac{\text{total annual production}}{\text{no. of persons employed}}\right)$$

| Industry | Unit | Output per person | | $\dfrac{B}{A}$ |
		Japan 1956 A	UK 1954 B	
Cotton	1000	20.0	10.8	0.54
Rayon	pounds	9.5	8.9	0.94
Cement	tons	1210	1160	0.96
Steel-plating		111	123	1.11
^a Chemicals	pounds	940	1499^b	1.59
^a Machinery		475	882^b	1.86

Notes:
^a = value added.
^b = 1956.
Source:
Hisao Kanamori, *Nihon no Bōeki*, Shiseidō, 1961, Table 41.

TABLE 4.3 A comparison of labour productivity in Japan, the USA, and West Germany, 1977 (USA, West Germany = 100)

	Japan/USA	Japan/West Germany
Foodstuffs	42.3	47.0
Textiles	87.4	106.6
Clothing	54.7	–
Pulp	–	137.0
Chemicals	69.7	112.0
Oil products	77.8	166.9
Rubber	102.0	384.6
Leather products	95.4	–
Ceramics	151.1	207.9
Steel	210.1	263.9
Non-metal products	75.7	202.0
Metal products	97.0	280.9
General machinery	173.0	210.5
Electrical products	136.1	365.0
Motor vehicles	137.6	202.0
Precision instruments	85.0	114.9
Others	119.8	–

Source:
Rōdōshō (Ministry of Labour), *Rōdō Keizai no Bunseki*, 1980, pp. 24–39.

TABLE 4.4 Changes in the composition of USA-Japan trade, 1965-75
(unit $1 million)

	Japan's exports to USA.			USA's exports to Japan	
	1965	1975		1965	1975
Cars	34	2 281	Machinery	392	2 195
Two-wheeled motor vehicles	108	576	Wheat	131	543
Steel	509	1 845	Soybeans	179	854
Metal products	137	562	Cotton	137	276
Radios	104	389	Coal	127	1 687
Televisions	62	255	Timber	137	1 061
Tape recorders	43	256			
Clothing	143	156			
Synthetic-fibre products	24	121			
Total (including others)	2479	11 148	Total (+ others)	2366	11 608

All this suggests that post-war industrial development can be amply explained by a theory of comparative cost expanded to include quality and changes with time.

4.2.3 The Development of Foreign Trade and the Domestic Market

In the previous two sections we discussed Japan's industrial structure from the point of view of the international division of labour and the development of foreign trade. However, we must ask ourselves whether the effect of foreign trade on the industrial structure was really so great.

The economic self-sufficiency necessitated by the blockade during the war brought about a considerable change in Japan's economic structure. Exports as a proportion of GNP (and as a proportion of demand for manufactured products) were significantly lower after the war than before (Table 4.5). A comparison of the extent of dependence on foreign trade

$$\left(\frac{\text{total value of exports and imports}}{\text{GNP}} \right)$$

with other leading industrial nations reveals that Japan's degree of dependence is higher than the USA, but considerably lower than that of European countries. In the 1970s the USA and European countries'

TABLE 4.5 Composition of demand and degree of dependence on imports
1902–75 (% at current prices)

	Consumer goods	Investment goods	Exports	Intermediate goods	Demand	Dependence on imports
1902–11	47.8	12.0	19.9	20.3	100.0	14.6
1912–21	34.1	17.1	20.1	28.7	100.0	11.1
1922–31	38.3	11.1	20.3	30.3	100.0	12.2
1931–40	26.5	17.3	17.3	38.9	100.0	7.9
1951–5	23.5	11.7	9.0	55.8	100.0	2.3
1959–65	22.7	16.4	8.8	52.1	100.0	3.1
1970	17.1	14.5	8.1	60.3	100.0	4.3
1975	18.2	8.9	10.5	62.4	100.0	4.3

Sources:
Yūichi Shionoya's estimates in K. Emi and Y. Shionoya, *Nihon Keizairon*, Yūhikaku, 1973, p. 140. For 1970 and 1975 – Gyōsei Kanrichō (Administrative Management Agency) *et al.*, *Sangyōrenkanhyō* (input–output tables).

dependence on foreign trade increased considerably. In Japan there was an increase, but it was on a much smaller scale (Table 4.6).

However, this does not necessarily mean that there was not a close connection between foreign trade and Japan's industrialization process. We say this because first none of the raw materials used by Japan's modern industries are to be found in Japan. Therefore only by importing them and exporting manufactured products can the imports necessary for the domestic market be obtained. Second, although dependence on foreign trade is lower than it was before the war, this is the result of the extraordinary measures adopted during the war. If we look only at trends after the war we see that foreign trade and industry have developed at about the same rate. In fact, one might even go as far as to say that Japan's industry has been actually led by the development of foreign trade. Third, the high proportion of exports before the war was partially the result of the nature of the textile industry. In the cotton industry raw materials costs were very high and the value added proportion was low, while a special product like quality silk was diffficult to produce outside Japan. These two products accounted for a large proportion of pre-war exports. Fourth, the great changes in the composition of traded products suggested that there is a very close relationship between the development of foreign trade and that of industry.

We must also take into account that the choice of a criterion for an

TABLE 4.6 A comparison of dependence on foreign trade for six countries

	Total value of exports and imports (commodities)		Total value of exports and imports (commodities and services)	
	GNP		GNP	
	1970	1980	1970	1980
Japan	19.4	26.1	21.5	31.2
USA	8.5	18.0	12.5	25.0
UK	33.5	45.4	48.5	61.2
West Germany	34.3	46.2	42.9	57.4
France	25.2	38.5	33.7	^{a}50.2
Italy	30.2	45.1	40.8	56.8

Notes:
^{a} = 1979.

Re 1970/1980 $\dfrac{\text{total value of exports and imports}}{\text{GNP}}$

Per capita GNP – Y, Unit \$1000 (Keizai Kikakuchō (Economic Planning agency), *Keizai Yōran*) Population N, Unit 10 million people, Transfer costs

$D - \dfrac{\text{cargo fares} + \text{insurance payments}}{\text{imports (FOB)}}$

(Bank of Japan, *Kokusai Hikaku Tōkei*).
If we correlate these figures (at 1975 prices) we get:

$T = 55.62 - 0.27Y - 1.61N - 1.70D$
$(-0.14)(-3.58)(-1.38)$

$R^2 = 0.71$.
Source:
Bank of Japan, *Nihon Keizai o chūshin to suru Kokusai Hikaku Tōkei*, 1981.

international comparison of dependence on foreign trade is no easy matter. If we use income levels, the indications are that Japan's rate of dependence is lower than international levels.[4] We cannot, however, ignore factors such as transfer costs and differences in endowment of raw materials. If we take the data on leading industrial countries (for 1970–9) on income levels, population, transfer costs, (calculated by cargo fares and insurance payments + imports (FOB)), aggregate them and correlate them, the figures we get for Japan's rate of dependence on foreign trade are not especially low.[5]

What we should pay careful attention to is that the relationship between the development of foreign trade and the domestic market is a complementary one rather than a competitive one, and that this relationship stimulated industrialization and the development of heavy and chemical industries. This was also pointed out by Hisao Kanamori and Miyohei Shinohara,[6] and can be easily understood in terms of an expanded theory of comparative cost. The building-up of skilled labour and the rejuvenation of capital were not only vital to the development of the domestic market, they were also important factors in the development of Japan's new comparative advantage.

In the case of heavy and chemical industries, the parallel development of the domestic market and foreign trade is often regarded purely as the beneficial results of mass production. Probably just as important, however, was the increased efficiency of the companies that competed on world markets.

4.3 INDUSTRIAL ORGANIZATION

4.3.1 The Pursuit of the Benefits of Large-scale Production and Industrial Concentration

It is well known that in modern industries, and particularly in the heavy and chemical industries, the benefits of mass production are considerable. The relation between efficiency and size in the case of power stations and ethylene plants are two excellent examples of this, and similar examples can be found throughout industry (Figure 4.1). Estimates of production functions also suggest that cases of increasing returns to scale are to be found particularly often in heavy and chemical industries.[7]

This could have very serious implications from the point of view of industrial organization theory. Suppose that in a certain industry the benefits of mass production are extremely great. In that industry, therefore, the tendency will be towards a monopolistic situation, with a corresponding loss of competition. Is there not therefore a danger of the industry losing its vitality?

The concentration ratio of Japan's industries was very high before the Second World War, but after the war the 'Zaibatsu', Japan's giant business conglomerations, were broken up, and measures taken to reduce concentration. In the first ten years of HEGP (1955–65) the concentration ratio actually fell, and although it has been rising since the extent of the rise has not been so great. Generally speaking, competition seems to have been maintained (Table 4.7). Why was it then that although the incidence of large-scale production continued to increase there was no general trend towards monopoly?

One reason was that there is a limit to the benefits of mass production.

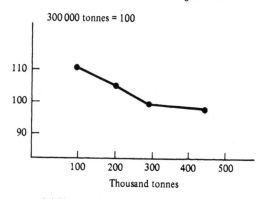

(A) The manufacturing cost of ethylene – index

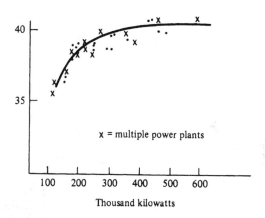

x = multiple power plants

(B) Generating capacity and thermal efficiency (electricity)

FIGURE 4.1 Efficiency and increases in scale of production

Source:
Keizai Kikakuchō (Economic Planning Agency), *Keizai Hakusho*, 1976, Table 3.29, Figure 3.30.

Even in areas where it is particularly beneficial, once an optimum size is reached, any further increases in size will not reduce costs significantly. From Figure 4.1 it can be seen that once plants reached a certain size further increases in efficiency were minimal. A second factor was that not all modern technology is suited to mass production. With new materials such as modern plastics, for example, the manufacturing process is relatively easy, and huge amounts of capital were not

TABLE 4.7 Changes in the degree of industrial concentration, 1950–80

	1950	1955	1960	1965	1970	1975	1980
Survey of 43 industries Base year 1950	100.0	93.5	91.5				
Survey of 170 industries Base year 1960			100.0	97.8	104.0		
Survey of 163 industries Base year 1965				100.0	102.9		
Survey of 327 industries Base year 1971					100.0 (1971)	99.8	100.2

Note:
The concentration ratio was calculated from the market share of the top three companies in each industry.
Source:
Kōsei Torihiki Iinkai (Fair Trade Commission), (1955–70 from Masu Uekusa, *Nihon no Dokkin Seisaku – Sono Kaiko to Tenbō*, but his figures are also drawn from the Fair Trade Commission's documents).

necessary.[8] Also the demand for an increased variety of products and improved quality tended to encourage decentralization rather than concentration. A third factor is that when the growth rate is high and the market is expanding, even if companies are trying to increase their scale of production, it does not necessarily lead to an over-all increase in the concentration ratio. This explains why there was no increase in concentration during the first ten years of HEGP. Even in a period when the over-all concentration ratio was rising (1967–72), in the industries that were expanding most rapidly the tendency was rather towards decentralization (Table 4.8). High growth is also beneficial in other ways. A high concentration ratio usually means high profits, but the correlation between the two does not seem to be so significant. An industry's growth rate seems to affect profits more than its concentration ratio.[9]

Finally, we must always be on our guard with statistics. For example, assume that the concentration ratio in the fast-growth industries and new industries falls, while the concentration ratio in existing industries rises. If concentration ratio indicators are calculated for a set number of products at fixed proportions, there will evidently be a danger of overestimating the rise in the concentration ratio.

During HEGP the domestic market was expanding rapidly, and companies were constantly joining the race to produce and sell new

TABLE 4.8 Growth rates and concentration ratios of different industries

	Change in production 1972 over 1967 (how many times increased)	Top three companies' concentration Ratio (%)		
		1967	1972	Change
Calculators	10.0	74.7	46.9	−27.8
Colour televisions	6.4	64.8	56.5	−8.3
Polyester fibres	3.7	100.0	59.1	−40.9
Styrene monomer	3.2	89.6	68.3	−21.3
Metal desks	3.0	47.2	17.6	−19.6
Oil	1.9	34.6	32.0	−2.6
Crude steel	1.6	47.1	59.6	+12.5
Paper	1.5	36.1	37.8	+1.7
Black and white televisions	0.8	50.1	54.6	+4.5
Cotton textiles	0.8	8.5	8.7	+0.2
Coal	0.6	32.2	51.3	+19.9

Source:
Kōsei Torihiki Iinkai (Fair Trade Commission), Documents.

products, so that competition was maintained. In the period that followed, however, the growth rate fell. Could we therefore expect growing concentration, and monopolistic trends? We will discuss the answer to this in Chapter 5.

4.3.2 The Development of Small Companies

While the heavy and chemical industries were increasing their scale of production, what was happening to small companies? Companies with less than 300 employees' share of the total output of manufactured products rose slightly between 1969 and 1979 (Table 4.9). In other words, small companies as well as large companies were expanding. That this happened in a period when the general trend was towards concentration, is particularly significant. These figures suggest that it was not a unilateral movement towards monopoly. How are we to understand this apparent contradiction?

Japan has always had a high proportion of small companies, and this feature still exists today. It has, in the past, often been regarded as a sign of the backwardness of Japan's economy, but it is doubtful whether this can be said even of the past.[10] In recent years, the more Japan's industry and society have progressed the more the proportion of small companies

TABLE 4.9 Small companies' share of total output of manufacturing industries
(figures = small companies' % share)

	1959	1964	1969	1974	1979
All manufacturing industries	50.6	49.4	49.0	51.3	53.2
Light industries 'materials' type	67.0	63.9	69.9	73.5	77.8
Light industries manufacturing type	78.1	75.6	75.6	78.9	80.2
Heavy industries 'materials' type	28.9	28.9	29.4	30.6	33.6
Heavy industries manufacturing type	39.8	39.3	38.4	41.8	41.0

Notes:
Small companies = those with less than 300 employees.
Light industries 'materials' type = foodstuffs, textiles, timber products, pulp, rubber products, ceramics.
Light industries manufacturing type = clothing, furniture, publishing and printing, leather, etc.
Heavy industries 'materials' type = chemicals, oil and coal products, steel, non-ferrous metals.
Heavy industries manufacturing type = metal products, general machinery, electrical products, motor vehicles, precision instruments.
Source:
Tsūsanshō (Ministry of International Trade and Industry), *Kōgyō Tōkeihyō*.

has increased. It therefore no longer seems reasonable to call this phenomenon the residue of Japan's former backwardness. On the contrary, we believe that we should think of these active little companies as part of the foundations of Japan's industrial and social development. (see Table 4.10).[11]

Their post-war progress has consisted partly of an increase in the numbers of the traditional type of small company – the makers of light industrial consumer products – as the economy has expanded, but it has not stopped there. In the 1960s and 1970s there was a major change in the composition of small companies, a shift from light to heavy industry. The number of different industries where small companies accounted for 70 per cent or more of total output rose from 340 in 1971, to 368 in 1977. In other words, they were competing successfully with large companies even in areas of advanced technology.[12] This, as explained above, was due to new trends in demand – for greater variety and better quality (especially where companies bought parts from other companies) – and the increasing number of manufacturing techniques where, because massive amounts of capital were not necessary, the trend was towards decentralization.

In this respect developments in the machinery industries have been particularly important. Let us look at a typical example. In the car

TABLE 4.10 A comparison of the position of small companies in Japan, the USA, West Germany and the UK

	Japan	USA	West Germany	UK
Small companies' share of manufacturing industries' output (value added)	58.0 (1978)	36.9 (1972)	44.1 (1967)	25.2 (1977)
Small companies' share of the retail industry's total sales	79.2 (1979)	70.6 (1972)	—	38.6 (1977)
Proportion of one-man or family businesses	28.5 (1979)	8.6 (1979)	13.5 (1979)	7.4 (1971)

Note:
Definition of small manufacturing companies – Japan 1–299 employees, USA – 1–249, UK and West Germany 1–499.
Small retailers – 1–49 employees.
Sources:
Keizai Kikakuchō (Economic Planning Agency), *Sōgō Keikakukyoku Shiryō*.
For one-man, Family businesses – ILO, *Yearbook of Labour Statistics 1979*.

industry, large companies have been able to exploit the great advantages to be gained from mass production. The manufacture of many of the parts for the assembly lines of large companies, however, is assigned to a multitude of small companies. This kind of division of labour explains why small companies' share of output increased in a period when the trend was towards concentration. The widespread existence of this division of labour, where the small company becomes an affiliated company of the large one, is regarded as one of the distinctive characteristics of Japan's industrial organization. In 1960 some 60 per cent of small companies were partners in some kind of subcontractor relationship with a large company, while 88 per cent of large companies had some of their parts manufactured by these companies.[13]

These affiliated companies are often portrayed as being entirely subservient to the parent company, which supposedly exploits their cheap labour and production costs for its own purposes, and uses them as a cushion against changes in demand. If this were true, the above-mentioned statistics on small companies' increasing share of output would be nothing more than camouflage for the increasing predominance of the large companies. We do not deny that there are cases where subcontractors are used because their wages are low and because they can be easily cast off if market conditions change. However, a high level of productivity and technology could never be hoped for from such companies. Furthermore, in modern industries, where quality control is such a vital factor, it would be extremely risky to be in any way dependent on such backward companies.

In reality, a great number of Japan's small companies boast a high level of technology and efficiency, and are valued by their parent company as a vital link in their organization. They are very often employed by the parent company because of the specialist technology and equipment they possess (Table 4.11). From the point of view of the subcontracted company also, the relationship is to their advantage; they can learn a great deal from the large company technologically, and about management methods. Furthermore, they are relieved of the necessity of searching for orders and can concentrate on increasing productivity. Thus fluctuations of orders and of profits are reduced. The

TABLE 4.11 Companies' motives for entering into subcontracting agreements

From the parent company's point of view

The smaller co. has specialist technology and equipment	47.0
They only need a small order	36.1
The smaller co.'s labour costs are less, so their product is cheaper	31.0
They can change the amount of the order more easily	29.9
They can economize on capital, equipment	26.8
Delivery and quality are very reliable	7.0
Because of capital or human ties	4.6
Others	4.2

From the affiliated company's point of view

They needn't worry about sales promotion, and can concentrate on production	42.3
Their amount of work is stable	34.1
They don't have to worry about bad debts owed to them	20.5
Their amount of work and profits are stable	13.6
The parent company's high level of management helps them to improve quality, design and increase output	10.1
They can learn technologically from the parent co.	8.9
They can receive help and guidance from the parent co. on finance and management techniques	8.6
Others	10.7

Note:
Because some companies replied affirmatively to more than one reason, the totals exceed 100.
Source:
Chūshō Kigyōchō (Small and Medium Enterprise Agency), *Shitauke Kigyō Jittai Chōsa*, Nov 1979.

picture of large companies exploiting their subcontractors clearly does not fit the facts.

As in the machinery industry, where the finished product is made up of several different kinds of parts (e.g. some electrical, some simple metal castings, etc.), the large company has three possible choices:

1. To manufacture everything within the company.
2. To buy some parts on the open market.
3. To subcontract the makers of certain parts (i.e. make them affilitated companies).

By always keeping these choices open, the flexibility and vitality of industry is maintained.[14] By letting the departments of their own company know that the other two choices are available, a competitive spirit is maintained within the company, while where the subcontracting choice is taken, provided the management of the affiliated company are given the freedom to be inventive, they will probably perform better than if they were employees of the parent company.

Thus these relationships reduce the costs and uncertainties that would be involved in competing on the market for the small company and also help to maintain competitiveness among the larger companies.[15] Therefore they can be thought of as one of the sources of vitality of Japan's industry.

NOTES

1. See Ryōshin Minami, *Nihon no Keizai Hatten*, Tōyō Keizai Shinpōsha, 1981, pp. 288–9.
2. Naohiro Amaya, 'Sōzōteki Hakai Koso Seichō no Hana', in *80 Nendai no Sangyō Kōzō*, ed. Nihon Kisha Kurabu, Nihon Keizai Shinbunsha, 1979, pp. 7–10. The opposite approach was taken by P. S. Heller in 'Factor Endowment Change and Comparative Advantage: The Case of Japan 1956–69', *The Review of Economics and Statistics*; and by B. Ballasa in ' "A Stage Approach" to Comparative Advantage', at the Fifth World Congress of the International Economic Association, Tokyo, 28 August–3 September 1977.
3. For technical progress and reduced costs in marine transport, see Yasukichi Yasuba, *Keizai Seichōron*, Chikuma Sobō, 1980, pp. 47–50.
4. Minami, *Nihon no Keizai Hatten*, pp. 177–9. Re industrial development and exports, see Miyohei Shinohara, *Industrial Growth, Trade, and Dynamic Patterns in the Japanese Economy*, University of Tokyo Press, 1982, pp. 12–14, 144.
5. A similar result was obtained previously by Yūji Hirayama. See Keizai Kikakuchō Chōsakyoku (Economic Planning Agency Research Bureau),

74   *The Contemporary Japanese Economy*

    Shiryō Keizai Hakusho 25 Nen, Nihon Keizai Shinbunsha, 1972, pp. 243–4.

6. Hisao Kanamori, *Nihon Keizai o dō miruka*, Nihon Keizai Shinbunsha, 1967, pp. 34–40; Miyohei Shinohara, *Keizai Taikoku no Seisui* Tōyō Keizai Shinpōsha, 1982, p. 7.

7. Iwao Ozaki made estimations of the production functions of all the manufacturing industries. He found that most heavy and chemical industries were on a large scale. See Iwao Ozaki, 'Nihon no Keizai Kōzō Gijutsu Tokusei to Shigen Haibun', *Chiiki Kaihatsu Nyūsu*, no. 98.

8. Kenichi Imai, 'Dokkinhō Kaisei no Konnichiteki Igi', *Kikan Gendai Keizai*, no. 16.

9. Masu Uekusa, 'Nihon Keizai no Kasen Kōzō', *Kikan Gendai Keizai*, no. 16, lists the major studies of the correlation between the industrial concentration ratio and profits as a proportion of owned capital:

Researcher	Period	No. of industries	Correlation
Ryūtarō Komiya	1956–60	46	0.07
Kazuo Matsuhiro	1961–5	35	0.54
Masu Uekusa	1966–70	35	0.34

According to an Economic Planning Agency survey, the relationship between the concentration ratio, the growth rate, and profits was as follows (1960–9):

	high-concentration ind.	*low-concentration ind.*
High-growth industries	27.1	34.2
Low-growth industries	20.6	18.7

Source: *Nenji Keizai Hōkoku*, 1971.

Thus it seems that while the concentration ratio is important, the effect of the growth rate of an industry is the decisive factor.

10. One factor that, it can be argued, enabled small companies to survive in the past was the coinciding of industrialization and the increased use of electricity. See Minami, *Nihon no Keizai Hatten*, pp. 101–2.

11. For a full discussion of this, see Hideichirō Nakamura, Tadao Kiyonari *et al.*, *Gendai Chūshō Kigyōshi*, Nihon Keizai Shinbunsha, 1981.

12. Chūshō Kigyōchō (Small and Medium Enterprise Agency), *Chūshō Kigyō Hakusho*, 1979.

13. Chūshō Kigyōchō (Small and Medium Enterprise Agency), *Kōgyō Jittai Kihon Chōsa*, 1976.

14. Kōnosuke Odaka, 'Shitaukesei Kikai Kōgyōron Josetsu', *Keizai Kenkyū*, vol. 29, no. 3.

15. It should be noted that as well as subcontractor relationships, other peculiarly Japanese organizations such as enterprise groups and trading companies also help in reducing these market costs and uncertainties.

5 Recent Developments in Industrial Structure and Organization

5.1 INTRODUCTION

In this chapter we take a look at the development of industry in the period since HEGP, and seek some hints as to what the future holds in store.

The joint blows of the oil price rises and the falling growth rate in the 1970s forced · a complete restructuring of industry and a drastic reduction of costs. The measures taken appear to have been successful, because Japan's performance in recent years has been better than that of most advanced industrial countries. In Chapter 3 we examined the adjustment process from a macroeconomic point of view; in this chapter we retrace it from a microeconomic viewpoint.

Around the late 1970s and the beginning of the 1980s, a silent revolution in electronics took place in Japan. In section 5.2 of this chapter we follow the course it took, and look at the development of the industries and companies involved. Finally we attempt to forecast what impact these developments are likely to have on industrial organization and macroeconomic growth in the future. We also touch once more upon the question raised in the last chapter, that is, why did industry not become more monopolistic and begin to lose its vitality?

5.2 INDUSTRIAL ADJUSTMENT IN THE 1970s

5.2.1 The Restructuring of Industry

By the restructuring of industry we mean the transferring of labour and capital, invested in certain industries, to other industries, in response to

75

changes in demand and the price–cost structure. The factors that made it necessary were:

1. The sharp rise in energy prices. This particularly affected the aluminium-refining industry and the petrochemical industry.
2. The stagnation of demand due to the falling growth rate. This particularly affected the companies in the steel industry, mostly small, which use the open-arc furnace.
3. The emergence of new industrial countries. This affected industries such as textiles, plywood, and shipbuilding.
4. The growth of friction with other leading countries over increasing exports, which affected particularly the steel, shipbuilding, and car industries.
5. The appreciation of the yen. While this did serve to offset the rise in energy prices, it also led to increased imports and made competition stiffer for exports. The expanding industries' growth made the yen stronger, and this meant that the weaker industries' ability to compete suffered considerably. Thus, under the floating exchange rate, the division into strong and weak industries became very marked. These factors were of course all interrelated.

Before discussing how the restructuring of industry actually took place, we will look at prices, production, and trade developments in the major industries of Japan, the USA and West Germany after the 1973 oil price rises (Table 5.1). The first thing that strikes us is that the impact of energy price rises was particularly great in Japan. The energy price rise itself was approximately the same as in the USA, but in relation to the over-all price rise, energy costs were much higher. The second significant factor was the development of the machinery industries, which have relatively low energy costs. Their expansion in both production and foreign trade was marked in all three countries, but particularly so in Japan. In the textiles and chemical industries of the USA and West Germany, price increases were lower than in Japan, and expansion was greater. In other words, because the energy structure is different in each country, the impact of the price rises was greater in different sectors. Also, because Japan was so dependent on OPEC oil, the need for restructuring was greatest in Japan.

Japan's reaction to the problem was a changeover from 'materials industries' to manufacturing industries. (For a definition, see Table 4.9.)

TABLE 5.1 The effect of the first oil price rises on commodity prices, output, and foreign trade in Japan, the USA and West Germany

$$\text{Relative prices} \left(\frac{1979 \text{ wholesale price of individual products } (1973) = 100)}{1979 \text{ wholesale price index } (1973 = 100)} \right)$$

	Japan	USA	West Germany
Energy	2.04	1.63	1.26
Textiles	0.76	0.73	0.90
Chemicals	1.12	1.05	1.03
Steel	1.04	1.11	0.90
Machinery	0.92	0.96	1.07

Output	(1979 *level*, 1973 = 100)		
	Japan	USA	West Germany
Textiles	105.0	110.7	101.1
Chemicals	124.2	131.1	116.1
Metals	108.7	98.3	94.6
Machinery	125.2	122.6	113.1

Foreign trade	(1979 *level*, 1973 = 100)		
	Japan	USA	West Germany
Textiles	164.5	260.3	199.7
Chemicals	281.1	321.5	282.2
Steel	267.1	179.1	221.3
Machinery	322.7	248.4	244.3

Source:
Bank of Japan, *Nihon o chūshin to shita Kokusai Hikaku Tōkei*, 1981.

5.2.2 Management Methods in the Adjustment Period

During HEGP Japanese companies concentrated entirely on growth, through active expansion of investment and employment. At this time, companies borrowing was increasing and the proportion of capital owned by them was falling.

With the vicissitudes of the 1970s the situation changed abruptly; they were forced to revise their investment, employment and financial policies. In the mid 1970s, when the anticipated growth rate fell, they began their efforts to reduce the equipment and employment they had built up because of their confidence in continued high growth. Also, with profits falling, they strove to make more efficient use of their assets. These measures (christened 'Genryō Keiei' – Keiei means 'management', Genryō means literally 'slimming'), had, we believe, the following results:

1. A reduction of costs, particularly fixed ones. Variable costs had of course risen because of the oil price rises, but it was fixed capital and labour costs, left over from when a return to high growth was still expected, that proved to be a tremendous burden. Because of them, the point at which companies could break even rose, so that making a profit became extremely difficult. Efforts to reduce fixed costs brought the break-even point down considerably (Table 5.2). In other words, companies learned how to make steady profits within the confines of low growth. Their methods had changed considerably from the 'Jitensha Sōgyō' of HEGP (literally, 'bicycle operation', so-called because when a bicycle stops it falls over, and if some companies were not constantly increasing their operating capacity they were likely to make a loss; such companies were of course always in danger of bankruptcy) when companies had constantly been trying to increase their scale of production. Also, because the required capital coefficient rose, the gap between the natural and warranted growth rates shrank.

2. The trend towards a falling proportion of equity was brought to a halt. Until the mid-1970s companies' proportion of equity had been consistently falling and was, by international standards, extremely low. From 1975 onwards it gradually began to rise (Table 5.2 (4)). The better

TABLE 5.2 Changes in the cost structure of Japanese companies, 1973–9

	Fixed costs as a proportion of sales (1) %	Variable costs as a proportion of sales (2) %	Profit–loss break-even point (3) %	Proportion of equity (4) %
1973	27.13	67.14	82.58	19.3
1974	29.81	69.02	96.27	17.2
1975	28.77	69.07	92.98	16.6
1976	27.76	69.51	91.01	16.7
1977	27.71	69.15	89.82	17.7
1978	27.82	68.15	87.36	19.2
1979	25.68	69.85	85.14	19.5

Sources:
(1)–(3) Keizai Kikakuchō (Economic Planning Agency), Nenji Keizai Hōkoku, 1980, p. 412.
(4) Bank of Japan, Shuyō Kigyō Keiei Bunseki, 1980.

companies especially varied their methods of raising capital – with stock issued at current prices, convertible bonds and so on – as well as increasing their internal savings. By increasing their equity they lightened their interest burden, thus making it possible to increase their internal savings even more. Some companies were able to make a profit with their surplus capital (e.g. by buying land and reselling it). Thus it is a mistake to regard all Japanese companies as 'over-borrowers'.

These adjustments naturally meant a considerable change in the industrial structure. These microeconomic adjustments could be said to have been behind the macroeconomic changes described in Chapter 3.

5.2.3 The Roles of Market Forces and Management Methods in the Adjustment Process

There are two views as to why, in Japan, the necessary structural changes in industry were achieved, and companies were able to reduce their costs successfully.

One is that it was the result mainly of the effective operation of market forces. The other is that it was the result more of the management and employment system. This latter view states that because of the life-time employment system and the seniority wage system (Nenkōjoretsu Chingin – wages depend on age rather than ability) employees have a very strong sense of belonging to the company. Unions carefully consider the condition of the company when making wage demands, and employees are not merely extremely co-operative – for example in implementing quality control measures – but also very positive in such areas as suggesting possible improvements in production methods. This 'company spirit', this view states, contributed greatly to improvements in energy conservation methods and reduction of costs. Thus the latter view concentrates on Japanese cultural factors such as social behaviour and organization, while the former looks at the issue from the point of view of accepted economic theory.

How, then, should we evaluate these two viewpoints? Rather than choosing one or the other, we believe we should see them as being complementary to each other. There is, we think, a need for further research into how far traditional social organization has seeped into the operation of the market.

Here we would like to consider how adjustments are made in wages and employment in Japan, as compared with the USA. Long service for the same company is not unique to Japan. According to Robert Hall, if there is what could be called a distinguishing characteristic of the USA economy, it is the long-term employment contracts system.[1] What is interesting, however, is that in the USA long-term employment is one of the factors that causes inflexibility of wages, whereas Japan's lifetime employment system has precisely the opposite effect. How are we to account for this?

The two terms sound very similar, and the systems are alike in the sense that age generally means better wages and conditions. In the USA, however, although the jobs of those employees who have been with their company a long time and attained a position of seniority, high wages and good working hours are of course guaranteed, for those who have not achieved these things, there is always the risk of redundancy. Under Japan's lifetime employment system there is virtually no danger of redundancy for regular employees. In Japan adjustment of the volume of employment is achieved by the use of irregular employees (i.e. those not employed on a lifetime basis) and subcontracting. Naturally, the safer regular employees' jobs are, the greater irregular employees' jobs are at risk. For regular employees also, changes in working hours, relocation (to a position they may have had no experience in, and for which they must undergo new training), and leaving vacancies unfilled (so that everyone in the department involved must do the extra work) are all carried out when it suits the company's needs. Thus we could say that in the USA system wages are inflexible and employment is flexible, whereas in Japan wages are adjustable but employment is relatively inflexible (see Figure 5.1). Put another way, the USA system puts adjustments of the number of employees first, whereas in Japan the emphasis is on adjustment of wages. It requires no complicated calculations to see that from the point of view of economic performance, a wage-adjustment-based system has advantages.

The speed of economic adjustment is affected not only by these differences, but also by factors such as market trends and households' behaviour. In fact what really decides adjustments of working hours and wages in Japan is market forces. Only 30 per cent of the employees of large companies are members of unions. The management always retains the choice of whether to manufacture something within the company, or subcontract to one of the multitude of small companies. This brings a strong element of competition into regular employees' working lives, because ordering parts outside the company could mean relocation for the workers of the department involved. In the same way such developments as introduction of labour-saving equipment influences bargaining between management and employees. To emphasize only the subservience and loyalty of Japanese workers, and to disregard

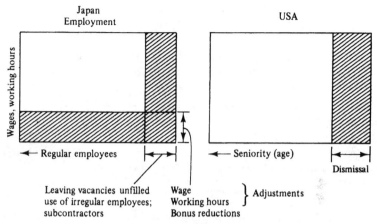

FIGURE 5.1 A comparison of the adjustment of wages and employment in Japan and the USA

the role of market forces, is a very one-sided way of looking at the situation.

There are also differences between households' attitudes to work in Japan and the USA. According to Hall, what US households seek most in long-term employment contracts is stability of wages and working hours.[2] In contrast, Japanese households tend to be very forbearing about fluctuations in working hours, and appear to prefer bonus systems and special allowances, despite the uncertainties involved. In this respect they could be said to be taking part in the risk-sharing of the company. Another feature of Japanese behaviour is that when irregular married female employees' contracts are not renewed they tend simply to become 'regular' housewives and do not appear in the unemployment figures (at least this was certainly true in the 1970s). This was an important reason why although under 'Genryō Keiei' unemployment did increase, unemployment figures did not rise significantly.[3]

The interpretation of household behaviour, both economically and psychologically, is an area that is still relatively unexplored.

5.3 EXPANDING INDUSTRIES AND COMPANIES OF RECENT YEARS

5.3.1 High-growth Industries of Recent Years

Even during the difficult adjustment period of the 1970s a few companies and industries were expanding steadily. Those connected with electronics and fine chemicals have expanded particularly rapidly, because of the technological revolution that has been taking place in these fields (see Table 5.3).

Mining and manufacturing industries expanded from 100 in 1975 (base year) to 142 in 1980, an annual growth rate of 7.4 per cent. A detailed breakdown reveals that during this period 10 out of 99 of these industries doubled their production. The electronics industry (electrical components for communications equipment, electronic calculators, etc.) and the manufacture of machinery and equipment that incorporate electronic components (NC (numerical control) machine tools, quartz clocks and watches) have been the main growth areas.

5.3.2 High-growth Companies of Recent Years

Next let us look at the companies that have expanded rapidly during the low-growth era, and see what distinguishes them.

Table 5.4 is a list of stock-market listed companies which, in 1975–9, not only managed to avoid making a loss, but in fact expanded their sales by 15 per cent or more annually. It is dangerous to make

TABLE 5.3 High-growth industries, 1975–80 (industries that doubled their production during these five years)

Industry	Production level (1975 = 100)	Examples of products
Metal-working machinery	214.6	Machine tools
Office-use machinery	406.6	Calculators, copying machines
Refrigerators, etc.	234.9	Refrigerators, car air conditioners, refrigerated show cases
Electronic communications equipment, components	289.0	Integrated circuits, transister diodes
Electronic calculators	228.7	External memory stores, input/output devices, terminals
Other electronics-applied equipment	2161.1	Magnetic recording and video equipment
Two-wheeled motor vehicles	205.0	
Optical instruments and components	200.2	Cameras, projectors, interchangeable lenses
Watches and clocks	542.9	
Photosensitive materials	235.2	Films, photographic paper

Source:
Tsūshō Sangyō Shō (Ministry of International Trade and Industry), *Tsūsan Tōkei.*

TABLE 5.4 High-growth companies, 1975–9

	Average annual rate of increase in sales %	Capital assets	Borrowings	Products	Comments
		(unit ¥ 1 million)			
1	18.6	870	3 195	Chocolate, cakes, ice-cream, sweets	Long-established company.
2	23.8	5 009	4 292	Ham, meat products	Strong because sells directly to the customers; now diversifying products.
3	16.9	32 120	9 714	Beer, soft drinks	Has biggest share of market because of excellence of products; sound management.
4	18.0	420	0	Oils, fats, chemical and synthetic products	Specializes in refining raw cotton seed oil; sales entrusted to affiliated company.
5	15.7	3 314	0	Synthetic resin products	Virtual monopoly in PVC piping, also makes resin products for cars.
6	18.1	1 920	0	Hormone drugs, enzyme drugs	Medical products specialists. Develop a high proportion of products themselves. Now producing medical appliances.
7	15.5	1 430	5 465	Rubber parts for cars	Member of Nissan Group; increasing their range of products.
8	16.6	3 300	20 044	Cathode ray tubes and parts	Cathode ray tubes main product, but now diversifying.
9	15.2	1 100	4 567	Civil engineering (esp. bridges), construction	Affiliated company of Mitsubishi; 50 % of business public works; also operating overseas.
10	18.3	8 200	27 748	Cans, plastic products	Has over half market of cans for food.
11	20.8	600	3 370	Pylons, steel structures, metal parts for aerial wiring	Leading manufacturer of pylons.
12	15.7	1 320	5 412	Induction hardening, Induction-hardened products	Does hardening of car parts, exports hardening plants.

(Contd.)

TABLE 5.4 (Contd.)

	Average annual rate of increase in sales %	Capital assets	Borrowings (unit ¥ 1 million)	Products	Comments
13	18.2	5 237	2 000	Forging machines, band saws	Top maker of small and medium-size presses, sales promotion excellent.
14	19.7	2 076	2 484	NC milling machines, orthodox milling machines	Leading company in casting; expanding overseas.
15	18.5	1 637	926	Diamond wheels	Leading maker of diamond tools, imports raw materials directly.
16	18.0	2 120	0	Machine tools, car parts	Top specialist in machine tools; affiliated company of Toyota; now converting to NC.
17	19.8	2 649	8 269	Car air conditioners, refrigerators, automatic vending machines	Concentrating on mass production of air conditioners, combustors.
18	15.5	2 499	0	Electric-powered tools	Top maker of electric-powered woodworking tools. Has affiliated sales company overseas.
19	15.7	1 625	81	Car parts	Affiliated company of Toyota; top maker of switches, locks, safety belts.
20	16.3	760	3 204	Synthetic resin paints, sound-proof materials	Very advanced technologically; produces electronic car parts, soundproof paint for cars.
21	19.6	1 650	3 139	Chemicals, building materials	Bactericides for swimming pools, Imidazole; now makes gates, developing derivatives of Imidazole.
22	19.4	585	350	Precision motors	Affiliated to Hitachi; specialist in miniature motors; produces DD motors for computer fans.
23	17.4	22 460	16 810	Electrical and electronic appliances, industrial machines	Leading maker of desk-top calculators, ECR semi-conductors; expanding overseas.
24	15.5	7 326	1 852	Audio and video appliances, TV sets	Developers of video technology, long history in audio equipment.

25	27.5	2 364	0	Magnetic tape, dry batteries	Affiliated company of Hitachi, Japan's third largest maker of magnetic tape (main product). Also producing electric shavers.
26	15.8	3 408	807	Desk-top calculators, computers, electronic clocks and watches	Top maker of desk-top calculators, leading maker of digital watches. Expanding in south-east Asia.
27	36.2	2 041	1 264	NC equipment and machine tools	World's largest manufacturer of NC machine-tool equipment. Manufacturing overseas.
28	30.2	3 000	0	Electronic equipment, car parts, jewellery	Advanced technology, ceramics for electronics industry
29	31.7	658	4 292	Car parts, electrical fittings	Car air conditioners and electrical parts, subcontractor of various 'pressed' parts.
30	24.2	715	628	Integrated circuits, film resistors	Top maker of high-quality fixed resistors, majority of products for non-industrial use. Taking part in joint venture with South Korean company.
31	21.9	1 848	1 227	Aluminium electrolytic condensers	Leading maker of electrolytic condensers. Has audio equipment factory and sales company in USA. Expanding in Singapore.
32	15.3	599	709	Motors, control devices	Affiliated company of Nissan. Makes control devices for cars.
33	18.2	13 176	59 086	Cars, buses, aircraft	Advanced technology. Leading maker of small cars.
34	17.9	3 303	11 960	Car parts	Affiliated company of Nissan, general car parts.
35	15.3	5 881	10 178	Cameras and fittings, office machinery	Makes all parts for own cameras. Now making copying machines.
36	16.1	800	4 500	Watches and parts	Big exporter, especially of 'decorative' watches. Expanding in Hong Kong.

Notes:
Capital assets and borrowings are for March 1979.
The companies on this list are those who report their annual results in the first quarter of the year, which increased their sales by 15% or more annually during March 1975–March 1979. Companies that recorded a current account deficit at any time during the period are excluded.
Source:
Tōyō Keizai Shinpōsha, *Kaisha Shikihō*, 1975–9.

generalizations from such a short list, but we think that the following picture does emerge:

1. Products. Common ones are parts and finished products of electronics-related industries and the car industry (especially makers of new materials, e.g. 'new ceramics'), labour-saving machinery and parts, and high-quality luxury products. Many of these companies manufacture virtually unique products, and thus can gain a very large share of the market. Finally, since the government recommenced taking measures to stimulate demand (1978–9), many construction companies have joined the high-growth group.

2. Capital assets. Most of them are relatively small. Of the thirty-six in Table 5.4, nine have capital assets of less than ¥ 1000 million, twenty-one less than ¥ 2500 million, and only three have more than ¥ 10 000 million. Generally their proportion of equity is very high, and of borrowed capital low. It has been said that the reverse of this (a high proportion of borrowed capital) is a characteristic of Japanese companies, and this has been the secret of their high growth. This list demonstrates clearly that this is not the case. There are seven companies with no loans at all, and nineteen with greater capital assets than borrowings. (In Japan such companies are rare.)

3. Technology. Many of them have developed a very advanced level of technology.

4. Markets. Many of them are doing their utmost to make inroads into foreign markets.

As was said above, many of the high-growth companies are relatively small ones. Table 5.5 is a comparison of the sales of different-sized companies. From it we can see that while the probability of small companies making losses is greater, their numbers include a higher proportion of high-growth companies. In contrast, large companies making losses are rare, but there are very few high-growth companies among their ranks. This is not just a recent trend in Japan, but rather a universal one.[4] During HEGP also the proportion of small, high-growth companies was high,[5] but large-scale, assembly-line industries such as the car industry, television industry, the shipbuilding industries, and the industries that produced their materials – steel and petrochemicals – also expanded significantly. In these areas mass production was essential for success, and this resulted in the growth of giant companies. A lot of small companies also made great progress because of new production techniques, but this development tended to be overshadowed by the growth of the large companies. Since HEGP the growth of the large

TABLE 5.5 The increase in sales of different-sized manufacturing companies, 1975–9

Capital assets	Total no. of companies	Increase in sales 1979–75						Operated at a loss
		Double or more	1.6 × or more	1.4 × or more	1.2 × or more	Same	Less	
Up to ¥ 1 000 million	176	5	21	13	20	15	1	101
,, ¥ 2 500 million	170	5	16	18	25	7	7	92
,, ¥ 5 000 million	87	3	12	14	9	8	5	36
,, ¥ 10 000 million	56	—	6	13	13	—	—	24
,, ¥ 20 000 million	42	—	2	8	9	2	—	21
Over ¥ 20 000 million	30	—	4	6	—	3	4	13
Total		13	61	72	76	35	17	287

Notes:
The increase in sales is for March 1979 over March 1975.
Capital assets are as of March 1977.
Even if a company went into the red only once in 1975–9, it is included in the 'operated at a loss' column.
Source:
Tōyō Keizai Shinpōsha, Kaisha Shikihō, 1975–9.

companies has not been so marked, and the achievements of small companies have been given more recognition.

5.3.3 The New Technological Revolution

As was explained in the last chapter, there were fears that when the growth rate fell, the number of new companies would fall, monopolistic trends would strengthen, and the economy would lose its vitality. However, even when high growth had become a thing of the past, this did not happen, and there was in fact significant growth among smaller companies. What was the reason for this? There were, we think, two main factors:

1. The increased demand for variety and better-quality products. During HEGP the majority of products were consumer durables and the same products were produced and sold in bulk. Mass production brought costs down so that they could then be sold to lower-income groups and, partly due to the demonstration effect, standardization increased. As incomes rose, however, and consumer durables could be afforded by more and more of the nation, the demand for quality and variety increased, and product cycles became shorter. Mass production could not satisfy this kind of demand. To take the opportunities for expansion that were occurring, companies no longer needed to be large. Flexibility (i.e. to change over rapidly from one line of production to another) was the essential quality in this situation.

2. Technological change. The technological revolutions of HEGP had been in mass-production methods – large-capacity steam generators for electric power stations, completely integrated steel works (thanks mainly to the introduction of large-capacity blast furnaces), enormous ethylene plants, and the use of transfer machines in the car industry. The technological revolutions of recent years have been characterized rather by the miniaturization of electronic parts, with the development of new materials. These are now used in such finished products as watches, cameras, sewing machines, and in industrial equipment such as robots and NC (numerical control) machine tools. It has become possible, on a small scale, to control separate manufacturing processes and variations in finished products by computer. In fact, this so-called 'Flexible Manufacturing System' (FMS) is now being adopted even by large companies.[6]

In fields such as the development of new kinds of energy, the resources of the ocean, and new transport systems, large expensive research and development programmes are essential in some areas. However, as these have progressed it has become clear that only by miniaturization and decentralization will steady expansion become feasible. Thus the distinction between large companies' fields and small companies' fields is no longer clear. These developments have made it easier for large companies to encroach on what was previously the province of small companies, and this may pose a threat to the development of the latter. However, this will mean fiercer competition and therefore will be beneficial to industrial development.

Next we will look at the effects of this technological revolution from a macroeconomic point of view. It has provided new investment opportunities and resulted in enormous savings of energy and labour, and these two developments have of course been complementary to each other. As labour and energy costs have fallen, capital's share of GNP has been maintained, and the investment ratio has risen. This has resulted in still further conservation of energy and labour. This process has been of vital importance for Japan's economic performance in the oil-price-rise era.

However, at the present time we are not in a position to make a final judgement. On the one hand, in factories where mechatronics technology is introduced it of course reduces employment there, but on the other hand it means expansion of the electronics and machinery industries and may therefore lead to an over-all increase in employment. Also, although the ratio of capital equipment has increased, labour productivity has also risen, so that the effect on the capital coefficient cannot easily be forecast. (The capital coefficient is rising in industry as a whole, but in areas such as electrical machinery, where technical progress is rapid, it is falling.) Thus only after the developments of the next few years will the direction things are taking become clear.

5.3.4 The Growth of the Tertiary Industries

So far we have concentrated on manufacturing industries, but in recent years the relative importance of tertiary industries has increased significantly (Table 5.6).

Some economists do not assess tertiary industries and their growth very highly. One reason is that their productivity is only improving slowly (Table 5.7), but their price increases tend to be big. The future, however, may see a technological revolution in the tertiary industries too, with the increased use of computers. It is very difficult to measure the productivity of tertiary industries. The problem, with services

TABLE 5.6 The increasing relative importance of tertiary
industries, 1955-80

	% of total domestic output	% of total no. of employed
1955	39.4	33.4
1960	39.7	36.4
1965	44.6	38.4
1970	49.4	40.4
1975	54.6	45.0
1980	55.1	47.7

Source:
Total domestic output, 1955-65 - Keizai Kikakuchō (Economic
Planning Agency), 'Kokumin Shotoku Tōkei Nenpō (old SNA), 1982.
Total domestic output, 1970-80 - Keizai Kikakuchō, Kokumin Keizai
Keisan Nenpō (present SNA), 1982.
(Both contain some gaps, making comparisons difficult.)
No. of employed - Sōrifu Tōkeikyoku (Prime Minister's Office,
Statistics Bureau), Rōdō Chōsa, 1982.

especially (though the same can be said to some extent about manufacturing industries), is how to measure the quality of output. There are
also difficulties on the input side where, unlike modern large-scale
manufacturing industries, working hours are very irregular.

During HEGP, because of the increasing activities of manufacturers,
the wholesale industry, financial organizations, insurance companies,
and repair and servicing companies all made great progress. In recent
years such fields as information services, design, and building management (i.e. cleaning, guarding and maintenance, especially of large
buildings occupied by several companies), formerly done by the
manufacturing companies themselves, have become the sphere of
specialists, and are now often carried out by a separate company. Also,
with the concentration of people in the cities and rising income levels,
reduced time spent on housework and increased leisure, the tertiary
industries dependent on personal spending have expanded. Finally, the
demand for better public services, especially social welfare and health
services, has increased considerably. Thus the tertiary industries are
becoming more and more important in the lives of the people. Their
price and quality are vital because they are a decisive factor in fixing the
standards of living of the nation.

Another vital function of tertiary industries is to provide opportunities of employment, especially for part-time female employees (see

TABLE 5.7 A comparison of productivity and price increases in different industries, 1970–80

Annual rates of increase	1970–5 (cy)				1975–80 (cy)			
	Increase in Output (real terms)	Increase in no. of employees	Increase in productivity	Increase in the deflator	Increase in output (real terms)	Increase in no. of employees	Increase in productivity	Increase in the deflator
Agriculture, forestry and fishing	2.5	Δ4.3	6.8	10.0	Δ1.9	Δ2.2	0.3	3.9
Mining	Δ1.1	Δ7.9	6.8	5.7	6.2	Δ3.1	9.2	5.6
Manufacturing	4.7	Δ0.3	5.0	5.9	9.4	0.7	8.7	0.5
Construction	5.5	3.8	1.7	14.1	1.3	2.5	Δ1.2	7.1
Electricity, gas and water supply	4.9	2.7	2.2	8.8	4.0	0.2	3.8	13.3
Wholesaling	6.6	1.3	5.3	8.6	4.6	1.9	2.7	1.3
Finance and insurance	10.4	2.6	7.8	8.0	5.9	2.0	3.9	2.8
Real estate	7.4	7.3	0.1	8.0	6.9	5.4	1.5	7.3
Transport and Communication	5.3	1.6	3.7	8.0	4.6	1.5	3.1	6.3
Services	2.9	3.4	Δ0.5	14.9	4.1	3.6	0.5	7.2
Total of tertiary industry	6.0	2.3	3.7	9.9	5.0	2.5	2.5	4.8
Grand totals	5.2	0.4	4.8	8.8	5.8	1.2	4.6	3.6

Source:
Keizai Kikakuchō (Economic Planning Agency), *Kokumin Keizai Keisan Nenpō*, 1982.

TABLE 5.8 The composition of employees in primary, secondary and tertiary industries

	Proportion of female employees Total %	Fulltime %	Proportion of part-timers %	Proportion of employees over 55 years %	Proportion of university and college graduates %
Primary	48.2	31.9	26.7	34.6	1.5
Secondary	29.7	22.1	10.5	11.3	10.6
Tertiary	40.0	32.8	11.9	13.4	20.7
Total	37.5	28.9	13.2	15.3	14.7

Source:
Sōrifu Tōkeikyoku (Prime Minister's Office, Statistics Bureau), Shūgyō Kōzō Kihon Chōsa, 1977.

Table 5.8). The development of tertiary industries has also widened for the female labour force.

NOTES

1. R. E. Hall, 'Employment Fluctuations and Wage Rigidity', Brookings Papers on Economic Activity 1980, I.
2. Ibid.
3. Akira Ono, 'Keiki Kōtai to Rōdō Shijō – Shitsugyōritsu no Hikannōsei ni Kansuru Hikaku Bunseki', in Sengo Keizai Seisakuron no Sōten, ed. Kenjirō Ara, et al., Keisō Shobō, 1980.
4. On the USA, E. Mansfield, 'Entry, Gibrat's Law, Innovation and Growth of Firms', American Economic Review, Dec 1962.
5. Keizai Kikakuchō Chōsakyoku (Economic Planning Agency, Research Bureau), Shiryō, Keizai Hakusho 25 Nen, Nihon Keizai Shinbunsha, 1972, pp. 171–2.
6. Yoshikazu Kano and Yoshio Tanaka, 'Robotto Kōjō Santai', in Kokumin Kinyū Kōko (People's Finance Corporation), Chōsa Geppō, Mar 1982. This is a fascinating factual survey of the electronics revolution, the introduction of industrial robots and FMS.

6 Japan's Financial System

6.1 INTRODUCTION

It is often argued that Japan's financial system has the following distinctive characteristics: (i) the predominance of 'indirect financing', and stemming from this – (ii) 'credit rationing', and (iii) the existence of an artificially low interest rates policy.[1] It is therefore widely accepted that the flow of capital takes place not on the open market, but at the discretion of banks and other financial intermediaries. By controlling these financial institutions the government is supposedly able to keep interest rates artificially low. According to Shinohara and Kawaguchi, the financial institutions carry out 'credit rationing' and have close ties with large heavy industrial companies, to whom they 'concentrate' their lending.[2] Banks' competition consists of trying to make long-term relationships with companies from all areas of industry, where possible making them affiliated companies of the bank. The behaviour of banks is seen as a vital background factor in companies' competition to increase their investment in equipment, and even as the motive power behind Japan's high growth. For example, Miyazaki argued that the attempts of giant business groups, led by banks, to cover the whole range of different industries and financial institutions, brought about an increase in monopolistic competition on commodity markets and in the financial world.[3]

In this chapter we will voice some criticisms of this way of thinking, especially regarding the roles of affiliation to banks for lending purposes, and government low-interest policies. We believe that even in Japan's apparently unique financial system, basic market forces are operating effectively. In the last section we look at recent developments and argue that the time has come for a complete liberalization of interest rates.

6.2 INDIRECT FINANCING

A comparison of Japan and other leading industrial countries shows that Japanese households save a greater proportion of their funds (except for France) and Japanese companies obtain a greater proportion of their capital through loans than those in other countries (again except for France) (Table 6.1). Thus one might say that in Japan indirect financing is more predominant than in other countries.

However, a closer look at Table 6.1 suggests caution:

1. The total amount of individuals' purchases of securities is second only to the USA, and, expressed as a per capita figure, the gap between the USA and Japan would be even less.
2. Although Japanese companies' proportion of externally raised capital is high, a large proportion of the capital raised by Japanese companies goes into investment in financial assets. If this amount is subtracted from the total capital raised, the proportion of externally raised capital is much nearer to that of other countries.
3. The value of Japanese companies' negotiable securities as a proportion of the total capital raised is third after France and the USA. The majority of stock issued by Japanese companies is purchased by other companies, while the majority of bonds are purchased by banks. However, in the USA also, private issues of stock (i.e. not through the open securities market) are not uncommon.
4. Japanese companies' dependence on loans has decreased sharply in recent years; it is now about the same as in the three European countries.

Thus we think that indirect financing can be regarded as a characteristic of Japan's financial system, but that the difference with other countries is one of degree, not of kind. Because the predominance of indirect financing is one of the basic assumptions of Miyazaki's theory and of the artificially low interest rate policy theory we should be careful not to accept them too readily.

6.3 THE BANKS' ROLE IN SAVINGS AND INVESTMENT

Hand in hand with the belief in the predominance of indirect financing goes the view that Japan's financial intermediaries, especially large banks, have considerable discretionary powers in deciding when and to whom they will lend, and that consequently their influence on the level of

TABLE 6.1 A comparison of capital circulation in Japan and four other countries (%)

	Japan 1974	Japan 1979	USA 1979	UK 1979	West Germany 1979	France 1979
Individual's use of their funds						
Currency and currency-like investment	14.2	8.4	6.7	2.1	4.6	21.8
Savings-type deposits	65.7	67.1	38.4	56.9	44.3	56.9
Insurance and pensions	14.0	16.3	35.4	40.9	18.9	8.4
Securities	9.6	9.1	19.6	0.2	23.1	12.9
Totals	100	100	100	100	100	100
	¥19.9 billion	¥32.8 billion	$211 100 million	£24 700 million	DM.120 500 million	F.239 300 million
COMPANIES — Capital-raising						
Internally raised funds	36.8	57.2	60.6	65.4	62.0	54.2
Externally raised funds	63.2	42.8	39.4	34.4	38.0	45.8
Borrowings	51.9	32.4	27.4	31.3	36.0	34.5
Securities	5.6	8.4	9.0	3.1	0.6	11.3
Totals	100	100	100	100	100	100
	¥25.1 billion	¥31.7 billion	$314 600 million	£25 800 million	DM.323 000 million	F.315 800 million
Use of funds						
Currency and currency-like investment	61.9	4.8	12.5	10.3	−4.4	29.5
Savings-type deposits	6.6	66.5	9.3	5.5	43.9	33.8
Securities	8.6	23.1	−0.4	70.9	32.4	12.2
Others	20.9	5.6	78.6	13.4	28.0	24.4
Totals	100	100	100	100	100	100
	¥4.4 billion	¥7.4 billion	$50 000 million	£2800 million	DM.33 500 million	F.45 900 million

Source:
Bank of Japan, *Nihon o chūshin to suru Kokusai Hikaku Tōkei*, 1981.

economic activity is great. They are supposed to dominate the business world, with the power to disregard market forces in distributing capital, and having a considerable say in the management of the companies they deal with. Thus they can supposedly influence economic trends by their decisions on which industries and companies they will lend to. Kawaguchi's and Miyazaki's hypotheses are both based on this view.

It is certainly a fact that banks play a vital part in the savings and investment process. We believe, however, that the above view exaggerates the extent of their power. In evaluating the importance of 'credit rationing' the following factors must also be taken into consideration:

1. There are twelve national-scale City Banks (as they are called in Japan, i.e. commercial banks), which is more than there are in most European countries, and competition between them is fierce.

2. The City Banks's proportion of both assets and deposits is decreasing, while that of local banks, mutual financing banks, credit associations, credit unions, life-insurance companies, and government financial institutions is on the increase. (The proportion of government loans to small companies and for housing is high.) The establishment of new branches requires the permission of the Ministry of Finance, and the smaller banks tend to be given preference.

City Banks do have the privilege of being able to obtain loans directly from the Bank of Japan. It is said that this privilege enables City Banks to persuade even large companies to 'affiliate', and to 'concentrate' their lending on these companies. However, their special position also means that they have to follow the guidance of the Bank of Japan, and this tends to check their activities. The fall in the City Banks' share of loans has brought into question the validity of Kawaguchi's 'lending concentration' hypothesis.

3. Transactions between Japanese companies are on a credit basis, so that until an account is settled the buyer automatically receives credit. The period is usually three months, but there are also cases of six, ten and eighteen months, or more. This means that investment is possible even for companies that have difficulty raising capital. Even if banks limit the number of companies they are prepared to lend to, capital slips through the net when companies allow each other credit like this, and the banks cannot prevent it. It is a factor that helps to make Japanese companies unstable, and bankruptcies common, but it does make it possible for them to raise capital without relying on the banks.

4. We saw above that the amount companies raise on the capital market, for example by issues of stocks and bonds, is not inconsiderable.

Stocks are issued mainly by expanding companies, and bonds by public utilities, and they are an important strategic source of capital for the companies involved.

Thus, even if indirect financing can be said to be predominant, banks face stiff competition from other banks, and from other channels of capital. Therefore we believe that their distribution of capital is in fact much less 'concentrated' than they would like it to be. This can be backed up by data on companies. Reports on the negotiable securities of 203 leading manufacturing companies (Table 6.2) show that while the actual amount that high-growth companies borrowed increased sharply, their dependence on loans fell, and their proportion of equity grew. This was because loans to these companies could be easily repaid from their internally generated capital and/or their increased equity. Also, the higher the growth rate of a company the greater was the income from its bank deposits. Thus lending to these companies was a very attractive proposition for banks. Figure 6.1 suggests that the more a bank traded with expanding companies, the higher was 'its profit margin. Thus as banks competed to lend to high-growth companies, the interest on their loans fell. Furthermore, the higher a company's growth rate, the less fixed was the order of banks they borrowed from (see Table 6.2). These facts conflict with the assertions in Miyazaki's hypothesis, and they suggest that expanding companies were able to free themselves from the necessity of affiliation, or other close ties with particular banks. The above data is for the years 1955–63, but the data in section (b) and (c) of Table 6.2, while fragmentary, suggests that these trends have continued in recent years. (The data in section (a), for 1955–63, was collected under the direction of co-author Yutaka Kōsai while he was at the Economic Planning Agency. Unfortunately this work has not yet been done for the following period.)

The picture of Japan's banks as omnipotent in the business world is a long way from reality. They may be able to dictate to companies that are no longer expanding, but not to the more successful ones.

6.4 ARTIFICIALLY LOW INTEREST RATES

It is widely believed that in Japan, interest rates, instead of being decided by supply and demand, are deliberately kept low, and the excess demand for capital which consequently occurs is dealt with by the banks' credit rationing. Credit rationing has supposedly been supported officially,

TABLE 6.2 Borrowing of companies grouped by their increase in sales, (a) 1955–63 (b) 1965–75 (c) 1975–9

(a) 1955–63, for 203 manufacturing companies

Increase in sales	Increase in borrowings	Increase in bank deposits	Deposits as a % of borrowings %	Ratio of equity %	Ratio of borrowings %	Rate of interest %	Degree of fixed order of loans from City Banks
8 times or more	9.57 times	17.4 times	49.9	38.7	32.3	7.88	0.681
5–8 times	8.27 "	8.73 "	25.8	26.7	35.5	8.3	0.705
3–5 "	6.59 "	5.06 "	20.9	28.0	38.7	8.34	0.796
2–3 "	4.31 "	2.86 "	15.0	31.6	39.3	8.5	0.787
Less than 2 times	2.74 "	2.19 "	21.1	29.4	39.1	8.84	0.808

Note:
Rates of increase (first three columns) are for 1955–63, ratios (columns 4–6) are for September 1963.
Source:
Keizai Kikakuchō (Economic Planning Agency), *Nenji Keizai Hōkoku*, 1965.

(b) 1965–75

Increase in sales	Chemical industry			Electrical machinery industry		
	No. of companies	Ratio of equity	Ratio of borrowings	No. of companies	Ratio of equity	Ratio of borrowings
10 times or more	11	15.4%	49.5%	8	37.8%	16.5%
8 times or more	13	14.5%	46.1%	9	23.2%	33.8%
6 times or more	13	13.5%	52.4%	14	18.3%	41.2%
Less than 6 times	9	12.6%	54.8%	8	19.6%	34.2%

Notes:
Increase in sales is for last quarter of 1965 to last quarter of 1975.
Ratios are for last quarter of 1975.
Source:
Mitsubishi Sōgōkenkyūjo, *Kigyō Keiei no Bunseki*, 1975–9.

(c) 1975–9

Increase in sales	Chemical industry			Electrical machinery industry		
	No. of companies	Ratio of equity	Ratio of borrowings	No. of companies	Ratio of equity	Ratio of borrowings
1.6 times or more	10	43.4%	8.6%	17	39.7%	12.7
1.4–1.6 times	13	21.8%	22.9%	13	18.8%	22.3
1.2–1.4 times	14	30.3%	32.7%	13	32.7%	20.7
Less than 1.2 times	9	25.6%	37.6%	5	28.4%	28.9

Notes:
Increase in sales is for March 1975 to March 1979.
Ratios are for March 1979.
Companies include only those that report their results in the first quarter, excluding those that made a current loss in the period.
Source:
Kaisha Shikihō, Tōyō Keizai Shinpōsha, 1975–9.

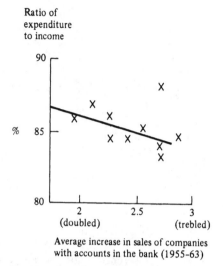

Ratio of
expenditure
to income

Average increase in sales of companies
with accounts in the bank (1955-63)

FIGURE 6.1 The relationship between banks' earnings and the growth rates of
the companies they deal with (first half of 1961, for ten major City Banks)

Notes:
Crosses represent the positions of the various banks.
The banks' loans to companies have been calculated from the securities reports
of 400 companies (excluding those of tertiary industries).
Source:
Keizai Kikakuchō (Economic Planning Agency), *Nenji Keizai Hōkoku*, 1964.

through the Bank of Japan's 'window guidance' – controls on the City
Banks' lending – and by regulation of issues of bonds. Figure 6.2
represents this process diagramatically. Because the rate of interest does
not settle at $\bar{r}_0$, but goes down to $\tilde{r}$, excess demand AB is created. This is
dealt with by credit rationing.

This is said to be possible because of the high ratio of indirect
financing. Instead of having to operate on the open market, financial
institutions can supposedly exercise discretionary powers. This in turn is
said to make government intervention easier. Recently, the financial
system has been in the process of change, and these so-called distinctive
characteristics are becoming less marked, though there are still areas
that have not been liberalized. These recent developments will be
discussed in the next section. Even with regard to HEGP and the 1970s,
however, the commonly accepted picture is an over-simplification of the
situation. Interest rates on deposit accounts, company bonds and

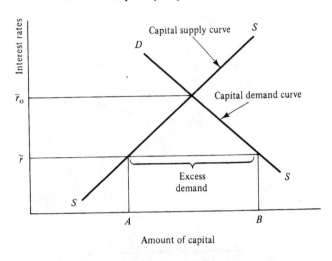

FIGURE 6.2 The artificially low interest policy

government securities were until recently rather inflexible, and City Banks' lending was limited by the Bank of Japan's 'window guidance'. To say because of this, however, that Japan's financial system was strictly regulated, that market forces did not operate, is erroneous. There are two major areas that are open to doubt and should be considered carefully.

6.4.1 Different Kinds of Low interest Policies and their Effect on Growth

There is a great difference between an artificially low interest policy and a 'general' low interest policy. The latter simply means increasing the supply of capital with the object of lowering interest rates (see Figure 6.3). In other words, low interest rates achieved by this method are the result of market forces, not a contradiction of them. If this policy is taken too far it can cause an overall imbalance of the economy, reflected in such ways as a balance of payments deficit or inflation. It will not, however, create an imbalance on the financial market. To put it another way, easy money measures, taken when there is no balance of payments or inflation problem, cannot be called an artificially low interest rates policy. When the balance of payments ceiling on growth was low, it was almost impossible to adopt a positive 'general' low interest policy. Thus the low interest rates of 1961, 1963 and 1972–3 were all relatively short-lived.

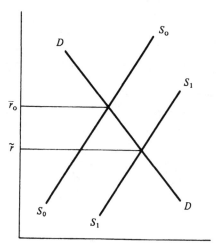

FIGURE 6.3 A 'general' low interest policy

In contrast, an artificially low interest policy is carried out by the direct regulation of specific interest rates. In other words, while a 'general' low interest policy's aim is to lower the market level of interest rates, an artificially low interest policy works by pushing interest rates down below their natural level. We emphasize this difference in order to question the feasibility of the widely accepted view that the artificially low interest policy promoted economic growth. As can be seen clearly from Figure 6.2, when interest rates were below the market level, credit rationing must have been taking place, which meant that the supply of capital was being restricted. It would appear difficult to describe a policy that restricts the supply of capital as growth-promoting. On the other hand, a 'general' low interest policy would, if it succeeded, increase the supply of capital (Figure 6.3), thus promoting growth, provided it did not cause balance of payments difficulties or inflation.

However, it is also possible to argue that the artificially low interest policy allowed investment in Japan's heavy and chemical industries to become profitable. Because they could attract investment in their infant stages, they were able to expand rapidly later. Looked at in this way the growth-promoting hypothesis is more feasible, but the following points must also be taken into account:

1. In the first half of the 1950s the profits of heavy industries were lower than those of light industries, but in the second half of the 1950s and the 1960s the reverse was true. Thus, even assuming that they did

need the support of low interest rates, it was only for a limited period.

2. Because of the growth of smaller financial institutions, particularly from the 1960s onwards, the City Banks' 'concentrated' supply of capital to large heavy industrial companies was to some extent neutralized.

3. Small financial institutions' interest rates were falling more quickly than those of City Banks. Gaps in statistical records make comparisons difficult, but in 1955 Mutual Financing Banks' interest rates on loans were about 2.5 per cent higher than those of City Banks, and Credit Associations' rates about 4 per cent higher. By 1980 the difference had shrunk to 0.4 per cent and 0.8 per cent respectively (see Table 6.3).

TABLE 6.3 Average interest on loans at different banks, 1955–80

	City Banks	Mutual Financing Banks	Credit Associations
1955	8.48	10.95	12.70
1960	7.72	9.94	10.29
1970	7.455	8.418	–
1980	8.273	8.710	9.085

Sources:
For City Banks – Research and Statistics Department, Bank of Japan, *Economic Statistics Annual*, 1981.
For Mutual Financing Banks, Credit Associations
  1955–Statistics Department, Bank of Japan,
      Economic Statistics of Japan, 1956.
  1960–Statistics Department, Bank of Japan,
      Economic Statistics of Japan, 1964.
  1970, 1980–Same source as City Banks.

4. It is generally accepted that interest on short-term loans has always been fairly flexible. Fixed interest rates have applied only to deposit accounts, government securities and company bonds.

It is true that the artificially low interest rates aided the development of heavy industry, but we can also say that the above four factors reduced the large heavy industrial companies' advantage. The overall result for the economy was probably the achievement of balanced growth.

6.4.2 The Effectiveness of Low Interest Rate Policies

The second major point to be borne in mind is that the artificially low interest policy was neither in force always, nor everywhere. In the early part of HEGP, there was a shortage of capital. However, when business conditions were favourable monetary policies were relaxed, and the Bank of Japan's 'window guidance' was suspended, or continued in name only. This was particularly true after 1965, when the capital situation improved. When capital investment increased and the balance of payments situation was healthy, interest rates fell without artificial regulation.

Furthermore, regulation did not extend to all financial assets. As mentioned in (4) above, interest rates on deposit accounts, government securities and company bonds were fixed, but call rates, interest on already-issued bonds in circulation and stock prices were not fixed, and they fluctuated considerably. Thus supply and demand operated on the financial market despite the restrictions.

6.5 THE LIBERALIZATION OF INTEREST RATES

As Japan enters the 1980s, its financial system is at a turning point. It is on the verge of a complete liberalization of interest rates, and the penetration throughout the system of the principles of competition.

We can divide interest rates in Japan into four main types:

1. Those that are allowed to fluctuate freely – for example call rates.
2. Interest rates on short-term loans which banks negotiate directly with individual customers. Most of these are linked to the Bank of Japan's official discount rate.
3. Regulated interest rates. Those for which the upper limit is fixed by the Temporary Interest Rate Adjustment Law (the Minister of Finance proposes a limit, the Bank of Japan Policy Board decides it in consultation with the Interest Rate Adjustment Council, and it is then announced by the Minister of Finance) or by the Bank of Japan's 'guide-line rate'.
4. Interest rates on issues of company bonds, which are linked to interest rates on government securities.

During and immediately after the Second World War interest rates were rigidly controlled, but regulation has been relaxed over the years. Interest rates on bonds, long-term loans and deposits are still regulated, but the merits of regulation are now undergoing a careful examination by the ministry of Finance.[4]

Similar reforms are taking place in other leading countries, and the powerful forces that have caused this trend are not going to make an exception of Japan. Let us look at the factors involved:

1. Financial and capital markets are becoming more international. As this trend progresses, the danger of artificial regulation leading to massive international movements of capital will increase.
2. Inflation. Because of continued inflation there is a considerable difference between real and nominal interest. The government can directly control nominal interest rates, but it is real interest rates that actually influence the economy. Regulation of nominal interest rates in a time of inflation does not have the desired effect, and it also tends to cause the money supply to accelerate, thus exacerbating inflation. As a stable money supply is one of the more important targets of the government's financial policy, it is wiser to allow interest rates to be decided by supply and demand.
3. The necessity for controls on government securities. Because of a desire to reduce the burden of interest, and in order to maintain the government's credit, issues of fixed low-interest securities have been common in the past. However, experience has shown that this makes regulation of demand difficult, and tends to lead to inflation.
4. Demands are increasing constantly for the abolition of monopolistic practices in financial circles, and the promotion of competition to increase efficiency. The fact that post office savings attract more deposits than private financial institutions has brought criticism of the latter's performance and the role of protective regulation is facing a complete re-examination.
5. Measures have been taken in recent years to liberalize interest,[5] but these could be said to be just the beginning. When the great numbers of government securities, now near maturity, come on to the market, liberalization of the interest rates on the bank deposits they compete with will probably be unavoidable.

These developments go hand in hand with general economic trends – the maturing of the economy, demand for a greater variety of consumer products, decentralization of industry, and the increase in the importance of the public sector – and we believe the future will see the active operation of market forces on interest rates and throughout the financial system.

NOTES

1. See *Gendai Nihon Kinyūron* by Yoshio Suzuki, a great authority on Japanese financial circles, Tōyō Keizai Shinpōsha, 1974. For recent movements see, by the same author, *Nihon Keizai to Kinyū*, Tōyō Keizai Shinpōsha, 1981.
2. This is the 'Yūshi Shūchū', literally 'lending concentration' hypothesis. See Miyohei Shinohara, *Sangyō Kōzō*, Shunjūsha, 1959; Mitsuharu Itō, 'Nijūkōzōron no Tenbō to Hansei', in *Nihon Keizai no Kiso Kōzō*, ed. Hiroshi Kawaguchi, Shunjūsha, 1963; Hiroshi Kawaguchi, 'Shōhisha Bukka Tōki to Yūshi Shūchū Kikō', *Keizai Hyōron*, 1963, no. 12.
3. This is the 'Wansetto Shugi' hypothesis. See Yoshikazu Miyazaki, *Sengo Nihon no Keizai Kikō*, Shinhyoronsha, 1966, pp. 31–92.
4. See Bank of Japan, Economic Research Department, *The Japanese Financial System*, pp. 48–59, and Bank of Japan, Research Department, 'Wagakuni ni okeru Kinri Danryokuka no Ayumi', in Bank of Japan's *Chōsa Geppō*, July 1977.
5. See Shoichi Rōyama, 'Kaikaku semarareru Nihon no Kinyū', *Kikan Gendai Keizai*, no. 45, pp. 18–19.

7 Social Changes

7.1 INTRODUCTION

Japan's economic expansion and industrialization process was accompanied by great social changes. We will first look at certain indicators for some of these changes.

The proportion of people employed in primary industries fell from 40.2 per cent in 1955 to 10.4 per cent in 1980, while during the same period the proportion employed in secondary industries rose from 24.0 per cent to 34.8 per cent, and in tertiary industries from 35.0 per cent to 54.6 per cent.

In 1955, 50 million people lived in urban areas, which represented 56.3 per cent of the population (total population 86 million). This rose to 75.9 per cent in 1975 (85 million out of 114 million).

In 1955 the average household consisted of 4.97 persons. This fell to 3.48 in 1975. This was largely because of the changeover from the extended family to the nuclear family.

Again in 1955, 51.5 per cent of middle-school children proceeded to high school (middle school 12–16 years; high school 16–18 years) and 10.1 per cent to university. By 1980 these figures had risen to 94.2 per cent and 37.4 per cent respectively.

In a quarter of a century, then, Japanese society had changed considerably in many respects. However, perhaps the most important feature of modern Japanese society has been the growth in the number of people who claim to feel that they belong to the middle class. The proportion so claiming has now risen to about 90 per cent (B + C + D in Table 7.1). 'Middle class consciousness' is felt by people regardless of whether they are farmers, labourers, or office workers, and it appears that Japan has become a 'middle-class society'.[1]

This 'middle-class society' is the result of economic growth, and at the same time the cause of the high rate of savings. It is also the key to explaining Japanese households' behaviour which has had an important bearing on the supply of labour. To maintain this kind of society, however, will entail several problems for the economy of the future. In

TABLE 7.1 How people felt about their own standard of living, 1965-77

| | *All* | | | *Employed persons* | *Farmers[a]* |
	1965 %	*1971* %	*1977* %	*1977* %	*1977* %
A/ Lower than average	3.0	3.5	3.2	2.8	1.3
B/ Slightly lower than average	17.8	16.5	14.6	13.8	9.9
C/ Average	47.0	49.0	40.5	41.0	48.2
D/ Slightly above average	27.0	27.1	36.1	37.2	36.0
E/ Above average	5.3	3.2	5.5	5.2	4.6
Totals	100.0	100.0	100.0	100.0	100.0

Note:
[a] Farmers are classified as self-employed.
Source:
Kōseishō (Ministry of Health and Welfare), *Kokumin Seikatsu Jittai Chōsa*, 1965-78.

this chapter we discuss some of these problems: the distribution of income, saving and consumption patterns, housing, and guarantees of security in old age.

7.2 DISTRIBUTION OF INCOME AND THE SPREAD OF CONSUMER DURABLES

The growth of middle-class consciousness could be seen as the result of the reduction in the inequality of income distribution, and a higher general standard of living. The starting point of this process was the 'democratization' which took place after the Second World War – the break-up of the 'Zaibatsu', the levying of a property tax, and the abolition of differential treatment for blue-collar workers and white-collar workers. However, to what extent is Japanese society really equal today? Also, in what way are these changes related to economic growth?

We think we can say that in Japan today income is fairly equally distributed. According to an OECD survey, Japan's pre-tax income distribution had one of the highest degrees of equality among leading industrial nations, and for after-tax distribution of income Japan was also in the top group (Table 7.2). Pre-tax distribution of income in particular is equal because the redistribution has been the result of labour market forces rather than a government redistribution of incomes policy. What is important here is that Japan's lower-income group is comparatively well-off. In other words, redistribution has taken

TABLE 7.2 A comparison of income distribution in Japan, Sweden, West Germany, the USA, and other OECD countries

	Japan	Sweden	West Germany	USA	OECD average
Gini coefficient					
Before tax	0.335	0.346	0.396	0.404	0.366
After tax	0.316	0.302	0.383	0.381	0.350
Atkinson's index of inequality					
∈					
0.5	0.08	0.08	0.12	0.12	0.10
1.5	0.22	0.24	0.30	0.36	0.29
3.0	0.38	0.46	0.46	0.62	0.50

Note:
Atkinson's index of inequality was calculated by the author, on income after tax.
Sources:
M. Sawyer, *Income Distribution in OECD Countries*, OECD, Paris, 1976.
The Gini coefficients were calculated by Toshiaki Tachibanaki, see 'Shūnyū Bunpai to Shotoku Bunpai no Fubyōdō', *Kikan Gendai Keizai*, no. 28, from Sawyer's figures.

place from the bottom upwards. This can be demonstrated by applying Atkinson's index of inequality. The greater the value of ∈, the more society is concerned about the low-income group, and hence conscious of inequality.[2] In Japan Atkinson's index is comparatively low when the value of ∈ is high, because equality receives a great deal of consideration. This is in complete contrast with countries where an increase in the degree of equality has been achieved by a reduction of the high-income group, leaving the numbers in poverty virtually unchanged.

The spread of consumer durables is often cited as an indicator of the 'equalization' of standards of living, and in Japan this spread was very rapid (Figure 7.1). This was of course the result of industrialization and economic progress, and is clearly related to the distribution of income. In the 1960s especially, the attainment of full employment and the weakening of the 'dual structure' of wages ('Nijū kōzō'), which had formerly caused a distinct gap between the high-productivity industries and companies' wages, and the low-productivity sector's wages, greatly contributed to the reduction of inequality. Meanwhile, the increased purchasing power of the masses expanded internal demand, and made mass production of consumer durables possible, thus spurring economic growth. Middle-class consciousness is thus to some extent at least supported by economic reality.

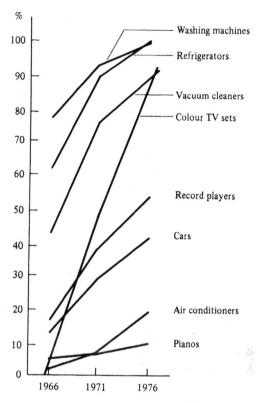

FIGURE 7.1 Diffusion ratios of major consumer durables, 1966–76

Sources:
Keizai Kikakuchō (Economic Planning Agency), *Shōhi Chochiku no Dōkō*, 1976.

There are, however, still some questions to be answered regarding the distribution of income:

1. What effect did the falling growth rate after 1970, and the changes in the supply and demand of labour that accompanied it, have on income levels? Assuming that the shrinking of the gap between the various industries' wages occurred because of the shortage of labour during the 1960s, the impact of the development of the 1970s on income distribution becomes particularly significant. There are some points that only the future will clarify. However, it is clear that during the inflation and long-term recession of the mid-1970s the Gini coefficient rose, but

towards the end of the 1970s, as adjustment approached completion, there was once again progress in the reduction of inequality. In 1978 the Gini coefficient of annual income per household was lower than it had been in 1970 (Table 7.3). Thus, provided that no great imbalance occurs on the labour market, it seems that it is possible to make progress towards equality even with a falling growth rate, and that it is economic disorders such as inflation and recession that cause the Gini coefficient to rise.

The fall in the growth rate has also brought about a change in consumption habits. During HEGP, partly due to the demonstration effect, mass production of the same quality and type of commodities was possible. In the 1970s, however, trends changed. People economized on commodities for everyday use, but the demand for high-quality, fashionable, sophisticated commodities increased. While maintaining the equality of a 'middle-class society', people were at the same time becoming more individualistic and selective.[3]

2. While the distribution of incomes was becoming more equal, what changes took place in the distribution of wealth? In the case of financial assets, the degree of equality in 1978 was actually much higher than that for the distribution of income (Table 7.3) which may seem surprising.[4] This is not the case, however, with non-financial assets (e.g. land, housing). Although we lack data on this question, most would argue that because of the rapidly rising price of land the trend has been towards greater inequality.

TABLE 7.3 Changes in the Gini coefficient, 1970–8

	Annual income	Savings balance	Net savings balance
1970	0.2669	0.3033	0.3075
1971	0.2748	0.3066	0.3159
1972	0.2705	0.3038	0.2978
1973	0.2736	0.3012	0.2948
1974	0.2711	0.2863	0.2687
1975	0.2742	0.2878	0.2789
1976	0.2771	0.2955	0.2916
1977	0.2760	0.2872	0.2743
1978	0.2655	0.2518	0.2256

Source:
Keizai Kikakuchō, Kokumin Seikatsukyoku, Kokumin Seikatsu Chōsakā (Economic Planning Agency, Economic Welfare Bureau, Economic Welfare Research Division), *Kokumin no Seikatsu to Ishiki no Dōkō*, 1979.

3. What role did the government play in the redistribution of income? As mentioned above, progress towards equality has been largely the result of market forces; the government has not been as active in this respect as has occurred in other leading countries. This implies that Japan's 'middle-class society' developed of its own accord, and did not need government support. In fact the people probably did not welcome government intervention. In the future, however, the population is expected to age rapidly as the number of children per family falls, and the changeover from the extended family to the nuclear family will probably continue. Thus the proportion of income allotted to areas such as government pensions is likely to increase sharply. Maintenance of the 'middle-class society' with an ageing population could be a major problem in the future.

7.3 SAVINGS AND LABOUR SUPPLY

We believe that the growth of middle-class consciousness in Japan can help a great deal to explain consumption and saving habits. As mentioned earlier, Japan's personal savings rate is much higher than most other countries. Paradoxically, this is not due to inequality of income distribution, but to the fact that the degree of inequality has been reduced. The people who save are not only managers and company owners; the rate of saving among ordinary employees' households is also very high. The 'equalization' of incomes, the growth of middle-class consciousness, and the high savings rate go hand in hand.

In the past, Japan's high personal savings rate has often been put down to such factors as a shortage of liquid assets, the poor welfare system, the difficulty of obtaining consumer loans, and the high economic growth rate. However, developments since HEGP have changed all this, and the savings rate remains high. This suggests that social and psychological motives for saving are very strong in Japan. According to a survey on these motives (Table 7.4), provision for the unexpected, for education (a major burden in Japan, see next section, 7.4), for housing, and for security in old age, were the most common. The average amount of savings that people were aiming for was ¥16 940 000, about 4.4 times the average annual income. When people were asked how important saving was to them 13.6 per cent said they would save even if they had to sacrifice a great deal, and 42.8 per cent that they were prepared to cut down to some extent. On how they went about saving, 43.1 per cent said they achieved it by cutting out all

TABLE 7.4 Japanese households' saving, 1970–80; objectives, motives, methods, and opinions on its importance

	1970 %	1975 %	1980 %
Motives			
Provision for illness, unexpected troubles	36.9	42.2	36.1
Towards children's education, wedding expenses	16.9	16.4	18.3
To buy land/housing (and repair the latter)	16.8	13.9	15.4
For security in old age	12.0	13.0	11.3
Others	17.4	14.5	18.8
Opinions on importance			
Prepared to sacrifice a great deal in order to save	22.0	16.1	13.6
Prepared to cut down to some extent	31.4	38.2	42.8
Save if money is left over	43.1	41.4	38.8
Enjoying life is more important than saving (and others)	3.5	4.4	4.8
Methods			
Cut out all unnecessary expenditure	35.1	42.6	43.1
Save a fixed amount each month	40.1	35.8	42.4
Save extraordinary income, e.g. bonus	42.5	37.8	43.5
Target			
Average amount (unit ¥1 000)	4 690	14 610	16 940

Source:
Chochiku Zōkyō Iinkai, *Chochiku ni kansuru Yoron Chōsa*, 1970–81.

unnecessary expenditure, and 42.4 per cent said by saving a fixed amount every month.

What comes out of all this is that for these people, having money in the bank is, in the same way as giving their children a good education, or owning their own house, one of the 'qualifications' of being middle class. Thus savings are not simply what is left over at the end of the month, but the result of careful planning and strong motivation.

How does the bonus system affect savings? In order to answer this, let us take a look at Miyohei Shinohara's hypothesis on bonuses,[5] and Hisao Kanamori's criticism of it.[6] Shinohara asserted that Japan's large bonuses (there are of course great variations, but usually they are paid twice a year, in December and June, and are, on average, equal to a total of about five months' regular salary) help to increase the savings rate, and that assuming bonuses are understood as 'temporary income', this can be justified from the point of view of Friedman's permanent income hypothesis. Kanamori said that bonuses were paid regularly, and they should therefore be included in households' anticipated income. It is certainly true that, compared with regular monthly savings, bonuses are very large. They are, as Kanomori says, included in households' anticipated income, but the fact that they are paid in a lump sum, over and above the regular salary, makes them ideally suited for saving. The point is not so much that the existence of this bonus system makes the savings rate high, as Shinohara maintains, but rather that households welcome the bonus system because it enables them to save more.

The growth of middle-class consciousness also affected households' behaviour in areas such as expenditure on consumer durables, as mentioned above, and investment in housing and education. In the same way it influenced the supply of labour. Hiromi Arisawa first discovered that the less the head of a household earned, the more members of his family were also likely to be employed (especially in low-income groups).[7] He pointed out that this tended to increase the supply of poorly paid labour, which of course depressed their incomes even further, and that this was one of the factors that helped to maintain the 'dual structure' of incomes. Even today there is an inverse relation

TABLE 7.5 The relationship between householders' income and the number of people in their families who are employed, 1977

Householders' income group (monthly)	Householders' average monthly income	Average number in household A	Average number in household employed B	% of household members employed B/A
less than ¥60 000	¥12 952	3.58	1.58	44.1
" ¥80 000	69 188	3.22	1.69	52.5
" ¥100 000	88 935	3.27	1.67	51.0
" ¥120 000	108 267	3.51	1.62	46.2
" ¥140 000	129 601	3.66	1.53	41.8
" ¥160 000	149 548	3.76	1.46	38.8
" ¥180 000	169 395	3.83	1.45	37.9
" ¥200 000	189 071	3.91	1.46	37.3
" ¥220 000	208 433	3.97	1.44	36.3
" ¥240 000	229 264	4.06	1.43	35.2
" ¥260 000	249 318	3.98	1.44	36.2
" ¥280 000	269 484	3.92	1.40	35.3
" ¥300 000	289 264	3.84	1.41	36.7
" ¥350 000	319 730	3.92	1.39	35.5
" ¥400 000	370 814	3.73	1.30	34.9
" ¥450 000	419 894	3.94	1.29	32.7
" ¥500 000	468 511	3.61	1.27	35.2
more than ¥500 000	650 422	3.63	1.12	30.9

Source:
Sōrifu Tōkeikyoku (Prime Minister's Office, Statistics Bureau), *Kakei Chōsa Nenpō*, 1977.

between a householder's income and the number of his family who are employed, but the slope is quite a gentle one (Table 7.5). Examined in time series this regression slope is gradually becoming less (Figure 7.2); in other words, 'multiple earners households' have become more common throughout society. Thus we think we can say that the members of the multiple earners households Arisawa talked about were working more to save the family from destitution, whereas today they tend to be middle-class families working to maintain or improve their standard of living.

The increase in the numbers of such families has of course meant a source of added income, and a breakdown of their expenditure shows that a large proportion of the extra income goes on the purchase of consumer durables or into savings. Thus the supply of labour is clearly

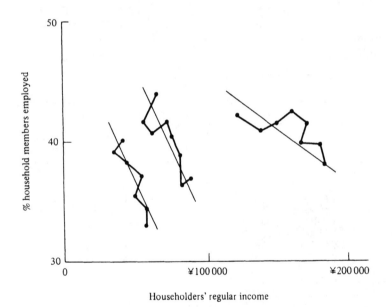

FIGURE 7.2 Householders' income and percentage of household members employed, 1965–75

Note:
The dots represent the place where the percentage of household members employed and householders' regular income meet, for each company size group.
Source:
Sōrifu Tōkeikyoku (Prime Minister's Office, Statistics Bureau), *Shōwa 38–50 Nen no Kakei.*

connected with increased savings, and both have contributed to the middle classes' maintenance of their way of life.

7.4 THE FUTURE OF JAPAN'S 'MIDDLE-CLASS SOCIETY'

With economic growth and industrialization, Japan has succeeded in creating an affluent society with a high degree of equality. However, this does not mean that there are no problems to solve.

A major one is that it is becoming increasingly difficult to maintain a middle-class standard of living. Working and commuting hours are long, and expenditure on education and medical care is increasing. Housing is extremely expensive, and the environment in many housing areas is most unsatisfactory. This is perhaps the price that has to be paid because so many people wish to give their children a good education, own a house, and therefore continue earning a high income.

These burdens have to some extent come to be shouldered by government expenditure. The government health insurance scheme now extends to all the nation. (Employees of small companies and self-employed people are covered directly by the government scheme, while companies above a certain size are legally required to provide a satisfactory scheme for their employees. The government subsidizes the former, but not the latter). The number of government schools has increased, but competition to enter university is very fierce, and many parents choose to send their children to expensive private middle schools (12–16 years) and high schools (16–18 years) rather than government ones, and to 'Juku' (private institutions that give extra schooling and special preparation for examinations outside regular school hours). Hospitals and surgeries are becoming increasingly crowded, and it is increasingly difficult to obtain satisfactory medical treatment without paying above the amount covered by health insurance.

The evils of Japan's housing situation have been exaggerated in some quarters, but it is a fact that the cost of buying a house in big cities is tremendous. Furthermore, housing development has taken place in a very disjointed fashion, so that cities and towns have tended to 'sprawl' and of course the urban environment has suffered. The government has not done enough in the way of low-rent public-housing schemes; in fact the only form of aid for low-income groups has been the provision of shelter for the destitute. The government's housing policy has consisted almost entirely of low-interest loans for people buying houses. This could be said to be a logical policy in that it caters for the middle classes' strong desire to own a house, but it has done nothing to reduce the actual price of houses.

Another problem for Japan's 'middle-class society' is the speed at which the population is ageing. It will be no easy matter to maintain a good standard of living for the aged in the future. Up until now their standard of living has been supported by improving salaries, as income became more equally distributed. As the population ages, however, the burden of government pensions and other payments will inevitably increase; in other words, equality, the foundations of the 'middle-class society', will have to be maintained by the intervention of the government. Thus there is the possibility that in the near future the foundations of this society may be shaken. Even if a redistribution of incomes between generations is carried out by the government, there are fears of an imbalance in expenditure because of the fast-ageing population. Old people in Japan have a strong desire to continue working, and also to live with their own children and their families. How the maintenance of the standards of living of the aged is to be shared between government pensions, family support, and income from employment old people undertake, will probably be a large social problem for the future.

Thus Japan's 'middle-class society' has its share of problems. Provided a reasonable growth rate can be maintained, however, and the middle classes retain their resolve, and the desire to improve their position, we see no reason why these problems cannot be solved and further social development achieved.

NOTES

1. For a comprehensive study of Japan's social-class structure see *Nihon no Shakai Kaisō*, ed. Kenichi Tominage, Tōkyō Daigaku Shuppankai, 1979. For an analysis of the political aspects of the 'middle-class society', see Yasusuke Murakami, 'The Age of New Middle Mass Politics: The Case of Japan', *Seisaku Kōsō Fōramu Kenkyū Hōkoku Shiriizu*, no. 5.
2. A. B. Atkinson, *The Economics of Inequality*, Oxford University Press, 1975, pp. 45–9.
3. For a very interesting view on consumption trends since HEGP, see Yuzuru Kamata, 'Shōhisha wa Kawatta', in Bank of Japan, Chochiku Suishinbu, *Chochiku Jihō*, no. 108.
4. See Yasusuke Murakami, 'Toward a Socio-Institutional Explanation of Japan's Economic Performance', *Seisaku Kōsō Fōramu Kenkyū Hōkoku Shiriizu*, no. 4, p. 81, note 33.
5. Miyohei Shinohara, 'Kōdo Seichō no Shoyōin', in *Nihon Keizairon*, ed.

Kōichi Emi and Yūichi Shionoya, Yūhikaku, 1973, pp. 79–81; and Miyohei Shinohara, 'Chochikuritsu no Nazo', in Bank of Japan, Chochiku Suishinkyoku, *Chochiku Jihō*, no. 127.
6. Hisao Kanamori, *Nihon Keizai o dō miru ka*, Nihon Keizai Shinbunsha, 1967, p. 100.
7. Hiromi Arisawa, 'Chingin Kōzō to Keizai Kōzō', in *Chingin Kihon Chōsa*, ed. Ichirō Nakayama, Tōyō Keizai Shinpōsha, 1956. This relationship was found to exist in the USA by P. H. Douglas. See P. H. Douglas, *The Theory of Wages*, Kelley & Millman, 1934, ch. XI.

8 Government Economic Policies

8.1 INTRODUCTION

Before introducing the content of this chapter, we would like to summarize briefly the preceding chapters. Chapters 1–3 examined the change from a high growth rate to a more moderate one from a macroeconomic point of view, and how the economy was beset by successive troubles – balance of payments problems, inflation and recession. We concluded, however, that generally speaking these problems were overcome, and that a relatively satisfactory level of economic performance was maintained. Chapters 4–7 examined the microeconomic 'foundations' that had made this possible; in other words, the factors that had enabled comparatively smooth adjustment, such as Japan's industrial structure and organization, company management, industrial relations, and households' behaviour. We suggested that what had helped most to maintain economic development in this difficult period had been companies' and households' adaptation to rapidly changing market trends.

However, many people, both inside and outside Japan, believe that the operation of market forces was stifled by certain 'unique' Japanese characteristics, and that economic progress sprang from other sources. The 'Japan Incorporated' (Nihon Kabushikigaisha) theory is a typical example of this way of thinking,[1] but such a view is untenable.[2] Far from being the outcome of the planning of a small elite, Japan's high growth rate was achieved only as a result of the high rate of saving by the people, by their will to work, and by the vigorous efforts of Japan's entrepreneurs.

There remains, however, the task of evaluating the role of the government. This chapter will consider three controversial issues: the objectives of government economic policy; the operation of the government's decision-making machinery; and the impact of the government's stabilization and industrial policies.

Government Economic Policies 121

8.2 THE OBJECTIVES OF GOVERNMENT ECONOMIC POLICY

It cannot be denied that the government has placed great importance on economic growth and the development of modern industries. However, this aspect is often exaggerated, and we are presented with a picture of an all-powerful government, sacrificing all other economic objectives for the sake of economic growth. Connected with this is the belief that in order to promote economic growth the government always gave priority to the needs of large companies. This view is unbalanced and mistaken; it ignores the fact that great importance was also attached to other economic objectives, particularly the distribution of income. A few examples will make this point:

1. Japan's effective corporation tax is about the same as the international average, but personal income tax is much lower than the international average.
2. It is true that large companies' effective tax burdens have been reduced by various tax exemptions. However, it is by no means only large companies that receive preferential treatment; taxes on agricultural incomes, for example, are low.
3. It is often pointed out that it has been government policy to give low-interest loans to large companies. This was true at the beginning of the 1950s, but in the 1960s and 1970s considerable state expenditure and investment went into housing and the improvement of the environment, and the recipients of low-interest government loans were agriculture and smaller companies.
4. Government waste, trifling unproductive subsidies, and misguided government intervention in the economy, have been under repeated criticism from HEGP until the present day.

These points suggest that the role of the government, rather than being the motive force behind economic growth, has been to distribute the proceeds of this growth throughout society as a whole, and to attempt to eliminate the frictions that occurred because of it. Certainly the idea that economic growth was the sole concern in all aspects of government policy must be seriously questioned.

It should be remembered also that government objectives have altered over the years. The titles of government plans reflect the changes. In the late 1960s there were 'Hizumi no Zesei' ('Correction of Imbalances' – e.g. consumer price inflation) and 'Shakai Kaihatsu no Suishin' ('Promotion of Social Development'). In the 1970s, as demands for improvements in social welfare strengthened, there was 'Atarashii

Nihon gata Fukushi Shakai no Jitsugen' ('The realization of a Japanese-style Welfare Society') (see Table 8.1). The establishment of an adequate welfare system could be said to be the ultimate objective of all economic policies and it would seem that a main objective of the government in the 1970s was indeed the establishment of a satisfactory welfare system:

1. In the 1970s external diseconomies such as outbreaks of environmental pollution, and shortages of social overhead capital, became marked.

2. Although the distribution of income became more equal, the transfer of income to those who were unable to work (the physically handicapped, the aged, fatherless families) was insufficient, and in property and assets the tendency was towards increasing inequality.

These factors made people realize that market forces served only to

TABLE 8.1 Major economic plans and their objectives

Name of plan	Year	Objectives
Keizai Jiritsu 5 Kanen Keikaku	1955	(1) Economic self-reliance (2) Full employment
Shin Chōki Keizai Keikaku	1957	(1) Maximum growth (2) Improvement of living standards (3) Full employment
Kokumin Shotoku Baizō Keikaku	1960	(1) Maximum growth (2) Improvement of living standards (3) Full employment
Chūki Keizai Keikaku	1965	Correction of 'imbalances', e.g. consumer price inflation
Keizai Shakai Hatten Keikaku	1967	Balanced and abundant economic and social development
Shin Keizai Shakai Hatten Keikaku	1970	(1) Balanced economic development (2) The achievement of a national standard of living in keeping with a powerful economy
Keizai Shakai Kihon Keikaku	1973	Improvement of welfare, international co-operation
Shōwa 50 Nendai Zenki Keizai Keikaku	1976	(1) Stable economic development and harmonious economic relations with other countries (2) A satisfactory national standard of living
Shin Keizai Shakai 7 Kanen Keikaku	1979	(1) Correction of economic imbalances (2) Energy conservation (3) The realization of a 'Japanese-style welfare society'.

increase the growth rate, and that a satisfactory welfare system could not be established without government intervention. Thus at the beginning of the 1970s 'Welfare before Growth' ('Seichō yori Fukushi') became a popular political slogan, and one even heard 'GNP Go To Hell' ('Kutabare GNP') in some quarters. Since the economic troubles of the 1970s, however, a more balanced view of the situation has come to be adopted. The present political trend is towards the above-mentioned 'Japanese-style welfare society', a different concept from the welfare states of Western Europe. What is envisaged is something based more on Japan's traditional social structure, though the exact form it will take is not yet clear.

8.3 THE DECISION-MAKING MACHINERY

Hand in hand with the view that the government has given economic growth absolute priority, goes the belief in a kind of 'general headquarters' that determines government policies, and whose 'commands' are carried out faithfully by all the various departments within the government. The validity of this latter belief is also very doubtful. The people who hold this opinion have different views on what this 'GHQ' actually consists of. Noguchi and others say that it is the Ministry of Finance and the Bank of Japan;[3] while most of the 'Japan Incorporated' group believe that it is the Ministry of International Trade and Industry.[4] These are of course powerful government organs, but their policies and organization are quite different from one another. Furthermore, the existence of sectionalism and rivalry between the various ministries and their departments is well known.

Another widely held view is that government policies are decided by government officials rather than the politicians themselves, and that these officials tend to support 'budgetary incrementalism'.[5] We think, however, that this view is guilty of exaggeration of one aspect of the situation. As was shown by Michio Matsumura's detailed study,[6] the officials themselves acknowledge the supremacy of the ruling party politicians.

Japan's ruling Liberal Democratic Party has clearly taken the leading role in policy-making. Major economic measures in the past have been pushed through by the strong leadership of politicians such as: Hayato Ikeda ('Shotoku Baizō Keikaku' 1960 – 'Double the National Income Plan'), Kakuei Tanaka ('Nihon Rettō Kaizōron' 1972 – 'Reorganize the Japanese Archipelago Plan', and 'Fukushi Seido Kaikaku' 1973 –

'Reform the Welfare System'), and Takeo Fukuda ('Sekiyu Kikigo no Keizai Antei' 1974–6 – 'Stabilization of the Post-oil Price Rise Economy').

The government of Japan is, however, not in the hands of a president, but a democratically elected parliament, and although the Liberal Democratic Party has been in power for a very long time it is by no means all-powerful. On such issues as the price of rice (fixed annually by the government), pensions, and the allocation of public expenditure (i.e. on roads, schools, hospitals, etc.), there is a great deal of pressure from groups of ruling party Diet members (i.e. MPs – Japan's Houses of Parliament are called the Diet). Because the ruling party is split into factions, it is easily swayed by the lobbying of pressure groups.[7] Thus, rather than any one aspect of policy being given priority, the tendency is to attempt to balance the interests of the various groups. Japan's tardiness in making decisions and avoidance of dramatic courses of action – for example in recent trade problems – is the result of this political structure. If Japan were really dominated by a powerful elite, such behaviour would be unthinkable.

While the business world is one of the more powerful interest groups, it is by no means overwhelmingly so. There are other very powerful pressure groups, such as the agricultural and medical associations. The unions too are powerful, but as they are generally company unions, their wage negotiations tend to have no central organization.

In conclusion we think we can say that the decisions on government economic policy are made basically within the framework of parliamentary democracy.

8.4 STABILIZATION POLICIES AND INDUSTRIAL POLICIES

8.4.1 Stabilization policies

Another factor that throws doubt on the view that economic growth was the government's sole concern is that, especially during HEGP, the balance of payments situation imposed a decisive check on growth.

One area in which the aim, method, and results of government economic measures was absolutely clear was in the repeated tightening of money supply in 1954, 1957, 1961, 1964, 1969, 1974 and 1979, yet these measures were of course in direct contradiction of the over-all policy. Economic expansion plans such as the Ishibashi cabinet's 'Sekkyoku Zaisei Seisaku' ('Positive financial policy', which aimed to reduce taxes by ¥100 000 mill ion, and increase government expenditure by the same amount) and the I keda Cabinet's 'Teikinri Kakumei' ('Low-interest reforms') were held up by tight money measures taken to correct balance of payments deficits (Table 8.2). Thus the government's freedom to carry out their economic policies was restricted during HEGP. In fact we could say that during HEGP economic policies were carried out not at the discretion of the government, but that they were governed by a set of 'rules' which had to be 'obeyed'. There were four major ones:

1. The fixed exchange rate of ¥360 to the dollar had to be maintained.
2. Monetary measures were to be taken when there were changes in the balance of payments situat ion.
3. The budget had to be balanced.[8]
4. The tax burden must not exceed 20 per cent of the national income.[9]

These rules all had different origins, but when they were put together it is surprising how much the run ning of the economy resembled classic capitalism. Having to maintain the fixed exchange rate was very similar to being on the gold standard; it meant that monetary policy responded

TABLE 8.2 Examples of macroeconomic measures that failed

	Year	Prime Minister	Measures taken	Result
Measures that clashed with the 'rules'	1957	Ishibashi	'Positive' budget	Balance of payments deficit
	1961	Ikeda	Low-interest policy	Balance of payments deficit
	1973	Tanaka	'Reorganization' of Japanese Archipelago	Inflation
Measures taken because of the 'rules'	1965	Satō	Policy of not issuing government securities (begun in 1949), in order to keep government expenditure down, continued.	Deepening of the recession (and eventually issues started in 1966)
	1969–72	Satō/Tanaka	Maintenance of fixed exchange rate/balanced foreign trade	Inflation (and eventually floating exchange rate)

automatically to the balance of payments situation. This, together with the budget and tax limitations, made the government really comparatively 'weak', certainly a far cry from the 'mighty government guiding the economy' envisaged by the believers in 'Japan Incorporated'. Moreover, the fact that the government was forced to set these strict restrictions on its own policies in order that Japan could survive in competition on world markets, indicates that Japan was still a 'small' country.

With economic policies restricted in this way there was of course difficulty in choosing suitable measures (see Table 8.2) and as the economy expanded and conditions changed, these 'rules' were gradually abandoned. However, mistaken government policies delayed the breakaway from them. In the spring of 1965 government expenditure was cut in an attempt to balance the budget, and this deepened the recession. In the following year the balanced budget rule was broken, and government securities were issued. At the beginning of the 1970s a chronic balance of payments surplus was forecast because of the continued maintenance of the fixed exchange rate, but a change in the parity was avoided and the old pattern of easy money simply repeated. This resulted in the massive increase in the money supply which was one of the reasons for the runaway inflation of 1973–4. From the beginning of the 1970s the balance of payments situation no longer acted as a ceiling on economic growth. This gave the government a freer hand, but their misguided use of this freedom contributed greatly to the tragic economic chaos that ensued.

Economic policies are no longer systematically restricted. The four 'rules' have been abandoned, and Japan is no longer a 'small' country. However, her high degree of dependence on world markets for both raw materials and imports and exports of manufactured products, and the people's strong feeling of repulsion towards inflation, mean that the stabilization policies still have to be carried out according to certain standards. Thus we could say that the situation has not changed fundamentally.

8.4.2 Industrial Policies

Another so-called distinctive characteristic of government economic policy is government intervention in industry. Through 'administrative guidance' ('Gyōsei Shidō' – government offices' informal guidance – from advice to 'strong recommendations' – to the business world) the government has supposedly been able to influence even the decisions of individual companies, thus greatly stimulating economic growth and the development of heavy industry, and fostering the growth of new industries.[10]

We think it is correct to say that on the whole understanding and co-operation between government and industry has been very good. However, to say because of this that Japan's is a 'planned economy' guided by an elite of government officials is going much too far. Japan's economic growth has been the result of a combination of the efforts of small companies exposed to strong market pressures, and the behaviour of Japan's households. These are not areas that can be regulated by the plotting of a handful of dominant figures.

Let us take a look at some factors that contradict the above view:

1. It cannot really be said that the government's protection of and intervention in industry has been aimed at the high-growth sector, i.e. industries in their infant stages, completely new industries. The government has had closer contacts with, and given more aid to, agriculture, certain smaller companies, and regulated industries. If we recall Japan's powerful political pressure groups, it can be seen that this is perfectly natural.

2. There are several examples of government plans which were not successfully carried through. In 1955 the Ministry of International Trade and Industry decided that there were too many producers in the car industry, so that production was on too small a scale. They came up with the idea of amalgamating them into one national company. This did not of course materialize, but in 1961 they tried, again unsuccessfully, to reduce the number of companies to just three. The secret of the car industry's strength has in fact been the unceasing fierce competition between the various manufacturers.[11] The 'Minzokukei Shihon Ikusei' plan – to foster the growth of national, as opposed to the giant international, oil companies – was also not a great success. The companies concerned have not developed as much as it was hoped they would. Thus, as well as the many successes in industrial policy, there have been failures, and more detailed research in this area would be useful.[12] Japan's macroeconomic plans tend to be 'decorative' rather than practical; nor can it be said that everyone agrees about the effectiveness of microeconomic planning, i.e. administrative guidance.[13]

We think that it is possible to say that government industrial policies have been successful in their support of industry as a whole, but that generally speaking individual companies have been left to cope with market forces themselves.

Industrial policy is not of course confined to actual dealings with industry. It is also connected with land policies, the preservation of the environment, protection of consumers and social welfare. Thus, before industrial policies can be accepted by the public, they are inevitably subject to a great deal of criticism and amendment. An excellent example of this has been the government plan to introduce nuclear power as a substitute for oil in the nation's power stations. These plans have been greatly delayed because of public protest, and what has in fact contributed most to solving Japan's energy problems has been the economies on oil consumption by companies and ordinary households. This episode has demonstrated clearly that the image of a powerful elite of government officials guiding Japan's industries is a far cry from reality; that the moving force has been the operation of supply and demand.

Of course government economic policies are important, and how skilfully they are executed can make a great difference to a country's economic performance. However, Japan, like other leading industrial nations, is a political democracy, and the government must work within the framework of a market economy. Thus there can be no question of the government being 'all-powerful'. Changes in Japan's international position, and domestic social changes such as the ageing of the population, suggest that there may be even greater restrictions on economic measures in the future, and that Japan faces an array of complex and formidable problems.

NOTES

1. J. C. Abegglen (ed.), *Business Strategies for Japan*, Sophia University, Tokyo, 1970.
2. H. Patrick and H. Rosovsky, 'Japan's Economic Performance: An Overview', in *Asia's New Giant*, The Brookings Institution, 1976, pp. 48–52.
3. Yukio Noguchi, 'Dissecting the Finance Ministry – Bank of Japan Dynasty', *Japan Echo*, vol. 2, no. 4, 1977.
4. US Department of Commerce, *JAPAN: The Government Business Relationship*, 1972.
5. This is mainly the assertion of Yukio Noguchi. See Yukio Noguchi, 'Dissecting the Finance Ministry – Bank of Japan Dynasty', *Japan Echo*, vol. 2, no. 4, 1977; and Yukio Noguchi, 'Yosan Hensei ni okeru Kōkyōteki Ishi Kettei no Kenkyū', in Keizai Kikakuchō (Economic Planning Agency), *Keizai Kenkyū Shiriizu*, no. 33, 1979.
6. Michio Matsumura, *Sengo Nihon no Kanryōsei*, Tōyō Keizai Shinpōsha, 1981.

7. For example, Prime Minister Eisaku Satō, who achieved stable government for a very long time. When he was negotiating with the USA about textiles, his policy in dealing with factions opposing the negotiations was to wait until the opposition weakened naturally, with time, rather than to attempt to persuade them 'positively'.

8. Public Finance Law, Article 4, prohibits the issue of government bonds to finance budget deficits (except those for public buildings). A special law has to be passed whenever this becomes necessary, i.e. permitting a special issue of bonds.

9. This was the long-standing policy of the government's Zeisei Chōsakai (Council on Taxation). See Zeisei Chōsakai, *Tōmen Jisshisubeki Kaisei ni Kansuru Tōshin (Zeisei Chōsakai Daiichiji Tōshin) oyobi sono Shingi no Naiyō to Keika no Setsumei*, Dec 1960; and Ryūtaro Komiya, *Gendai Nihon Keizai Kenkyū*, Tōkyō Daigaku Shuppankai, 1975, pp. 107–9.

10. It has long been widely believed that the Bank of Japan's 'window guidance' is a very important part of the government's financial policies. Recently, however, the effectiveness of 'window operations' has been questioned. See Akiyoshi Horiuchi, *Nihon no Kinyū Seisaku*, Tōyō Keizai Shinpōsha, 1981, ch. 4.

11. Toshimasa Tsuruta, *Sengo Nihon no Sangyō Seisaku*, Nihon Keizai Shinbunsha, 1982, pp. 168–74.

12. For a meticulous piece of research on adjustments in equipment investment in the iron and steel industry, see Yoshio Miwa, 'Tekkōgyō no Setsubi Tōshi Chōsei no Keizaiteki Kiketsu', *Shinshū Daigaku Keizai Ronshū*, no. 11.

13. Ryūtarō Komiya, *Gendai Nihon Keizai Kenkyū*, Tōdai Shuppankai, 1975, ch. 10.

Index

Note: all *italicized* references refer to tables.

Printed and bound by PG in the USA